# El Farol

# El Farol

## TAPAS AND SPANISH CUISINE

CHEF JAMES CAMPBELL CARUSO

Gibbs Smith, Publisher
Salt Lake City

08 07 06 05          5 4 3 2

Published by
Gibbs Smith, Publisher
P.O. Box 667
Layton, Utah 84041

Orders: 1-800-748-5439
www.gibbs-smith.com

Designed by Rudy Ramos
Printed in Hong Kong

**Library of Congress Cataloging-in-Publication Data**

Caruso, James Campbell.
   El Farol : Tapas and Spanish cuisine / James Campbell Caruso;
        foreword by David Salazar. — 1st ed.
   p. cm.
   ISBN 1-58685-101-2
   1. Cookery, Spanish. I. Title.
TX723.5.S7 C3563 2004
641.5946—dc22                     2003017119

# Dedication

To my family of passionate cooks; past, present, and future, with love and gratitude for the endless inspiration you give me.

# Contents

Foreword xi

Preface xv

Acknowledgments xix

## El Farol Basics
### 1

Sofrito, 3

Basic Aioli, 4

Lemon-Caper Aioli, 5

Aioli de Higos, 6

Aioli de Garbanzos, 7

Green Onion Butter, 8

Pesto Moro, 9

Cabrales Butter, 11

El Farol Preserved Lemons, 12

Preserved Lemon Butter Sauce, 13

Green Olive Vinaigrette, 14

Saffron Vinaigrette, 15

Chipotle-Mustard Vinaigrette, 16

Vinagre de Jerez, 17

Mojo Verde, 18

Pickled Red Onions, 19

Compota de Manzanas y Vino, 20

Moroccan Carrot Sauce, 21

Espresso-Chipotle Sauce, 22

Aji Amarillo Salsa, 23

Harissa Sauce, 24

Port-Fig Syrup, 26

Toasted Cumin Tomato Sauce, 27

Pernod Saffron Cream Sauce, 28

Mediterranean Salsa, 29

Romesco Sauce, 30

Curry Oil, 32

Paprika Oil, 33

Migas, 34

Salsa Verde with Fennel Seed, 35

El Farol Pincho Spice Mix, 36

Chicken Stock, 37

Jamon Stock, 38

Fish Stock, 39

## Sopas y Caldos
### Soups and Stews
### 41

Fabada, 43

Caldo Pescado, 45

Marmitako, 46

Oyster-Potato Soup, 47

Posole Clam Chowder, 48

Sopa de Guisantes, 49

Gazpacho, 51

Sopa de Almendras, 52

## Tapas Frias
### Cold Tapas
### 53

Betabeles, 55
Sandia con Jamon, 57
Mejillones al Vinagreta, 58
Mojama, 59
Jicama with Lime and
    Catarina Chile, 60
Goat Cheese Dressing, 61
Ensalada de Uvas con Queso, 63
Ceviche, 64
Bay Scallop Ceviche, 65
Salmon Ceviche with
    Sweet Corn Vinaigrette, 66

Mediterranean Couscous Salad, 67
Marinated Olives, 69
Marinated Peruvian Purple Potatoes, 70
Pollo Curri, 71
Preserved Lemon Goat Cheese
    Spread, 72
Queso Fresco, 73
Shrimp Escabeche with
    Black Olives and Mint, 75
Orange-Fennel-Olive Salad, 76
Moroccan Eggplant, 77
Tortilla Española, 79

## Tapas Calientes
### Hot Tapas
### 81

Espinaca con Pasas, 83
Gambas al Ajillo, 84
Bonito, 85
Portobellos en Jerez, 87
Pasta Piñon Verde, 88
Higos Rellenos, 89
Argentine Beef Empanadas, 91
Baked Oyster and
    Pancetta Empanadas, 94
Portobello-Cabrales Empanadas, 96
Chorizo-Potato Empanadas, 98
Gambas al Alcaparra, 101
Puerco Asado, 102

Albondigas, 103
Pulpo Asado, 105
Queso Frito, 106
Croquetas de Salmone, 107
Croquetas de Bacaloa, 108
Pinchos de Venado, 109
Pez Espada, 110
Almejas con Manzanilla, 111
Sardinas al la Plancha, 112
El Farol Fried Calamari, 114
Pollo Harissa, 115
Aguacate, 117

## Tapas Calientes
### Hot Tapas, continued

Achiote Citrus-Steamed Chicken in
  Banana Leaf, 118
Hojas de Uva, 119
Pimientos de Padron, 121
Pepita Flatbread, 122

Rosemary-Yogurt Flatbread, 123
Mejillones con Jamon, 125
Alcachofas, 126
Patatas Bravas, 129


## Main Courses
### 131

Paella de Puerco y Espinaca, 133
Paella Mixta, 134
Paella de Gambas y Morcilla, 137
Pepita-Crusted Salmon with
  Toasted Cumin Tomato Sauce, 139
Trout Wrapped in Jamon Serrano, 140
Zarzuela de Mariscos, 141
Puerco con Manzanas y Cabrales, 142
Beef Tenderloin with
  Cabrales Butter, 144
Rabo de Toro, 145

Roasted Duck with
  Moroccan Carrot Sauce, 147
Cordero Harissa, 148
Cod with Clams and Chorizo, 150
Carne Milanesa with Lemon-Caper
  Aioli, 151
Grilled Quail with
  Espresso-Chipotle Sauce, 153
Grilled Lobster with
  Chipotle-Mustard Vinaigrette, 154


## Postres
### Desserts
### 155

Chocolate al Vapor, 157
Higos y Datiles, 158
El Farol Goat Cheese Tart, 160
Lemon-Rosemary Flan, 162
Pastelitos de Dulce de Membrillo, 164
Lavender Goat's Milk Flan, 165
Orange Polenta Almond Cake, 166

Raspado de Sangria, 167
Torrijas, 168
Sweet Coconut Rice Pudding, 169
Torta de Chocolate, 171
Pedro Ximenez Caramel Sauce, 172
Milagro Sugar Cookies, 173
Royal Icing, 174

## Drinks

175

Nectar de los Dioses, 177
Sangria Tinta de El Farol, 179
Sangria Blanca de El Farol, 180
Melon Mezcalito, 181

Sangrita Oyster Shooters, 183
Carajillo, 184
Siesta El Farol, 185

About Spanish Wines 187
Pantry Items 191
Sources 195
Index 197

# Foreword

*David Salazar*
*Owner, El Farol*

On July 18, 1985, I bought El Farol, the oldest restaurant and bar in Santa Fe, New Mexico. El Farol previously existed under different names, but in 1968 Bob Young took it over from the Vigil, Serna, and Tapia families, and named it El Farol.

The Vigil family always had some commercial enterprise in what is now the bar at El Farol, and as with so many family businesses, the family lived in the adjacent rooms. El Farol had always been a place where the neighborhood gathered daily to share news about what was going on in the community. Canyon Road was a bustling small business area with grocery stores and even a gas station.

I grew up in similar circumstances in northern New Mexico, where my dad owned a thriving general store in Hernandez. Our home was also adjacent to my dad's store. I believe that I learned as much in my youth working in that store as I did in my formal education.

Prior to buying El Farol I had never worked in a restaurant, and the first months of my ownership were the hardest work that I have ever done in my life. Shortly after I bought the restaurant, Phylis Kapp, a local gallery owner on Canyon Road, introduced me to a friend of hers named Denise Dreszman. Denise was from New York City and was a chef at The Ballroom in New York, one of the first authentic Spanish restaurants in the United States. Originally from Toronto, Canada, she was a graduate of the Culinary Institute of America (CIA). Denise is responsible for starting the Spanish menu at El Farol.

Denise and I were the first to bring tapas to Santa Fe and New Mexico. It revolutionized dining in Santa Fe. Many customers came and shared tapas. Diners became more adventuresome because they were able to experiment with the small dishes. Sharing tapas also invited the social aspect of dining, which we continue to encourage at El Farol.

We also introduced Spanish wines on a grand scale. The wine industry in Spain has existed for hundreds of years, and our wine list is one of the best Spanish wine lists in this country.

I have been very lucky in having great chefs. We are still using some of Denise Dreszman's recipes to this day. Those who followed Denise are Ned Laventall, Kit Baum, and Genovevo (Vevo) Rivera.

For the last four years I have been fortunate to work with a superb chef: James Campbell Caruso, who has added great passion to the menu at El Farol. He is a student of Spanish cuisine and has traveled and cooked in Sevilla and Jerez de la Frontera. James came to New Mexico from Boston to study anthropology at the University of New Mexico. His anthropological training and love of cooking led him to explore the origins of Spanish cuisine and the different cultures that have influenced Spanish food. An El Farol cookbook has been a longtime goal of mine. James has taken this challenging goal and made it a reality. Great work, James.

—David Salazar
Owner, El Farol

*Clockwise, from left:*
*One of El Farol's five dining rooms in an 1835*
*adobe. A variety of tapas, or "small plates."*
*The famous El Farol bar, with frescoes by*
*Alfred Morang.*

*Clockwise, from lower left:*
Flamenco at El Farol, *an oil painting by Roland Van Loon.* Canyon Road entrance *and portal to El Farol. The Flamenco Room. The Tapas Room, with murals by William Vincent.*

# Preface

*Chef James Campbell Caruso*

El Farol has a long tradition of offering a unique dining experience in the lively and eclectic setting of an 1835 adobe. Big, bold, and interesting flavors are part of the colorful tapestry of the El Farol experience. The cooking methods included in this book are simple and straightforward, but this is definitely not basic cooking 101. As you approach this unique cuisine that combines contemporary and traditional foods of Spanish-speaking countries, you will find yourself using some complex flavor combinations and techniques you may not have used before—some that could get you thrown out of cooking school!

The rich and diverse cultural traditions of New Mexico, of course, have a profound influence on the foods and flavors of El Farol, but this is only the beginning. We are, in essence, a Spanish restaurant that serves tapas, paella, and Spanish wines. Sounds simple enough, but what does that mean in Santa Fe? Take into account the obvious Spanish influence on the food and everything else in this area.

What is Spanish food? The Iberian Peninsula has been inhabited by Celts, Romans, Jews, and Phoenicians, not to mention eight hundred or so years of occupation by the Moors. All of these cultures left their mark in the evolution of one of the greatest and most mosaic of all food histories. So, when Spanish cooks arrived in the new world, their recipe books were already bulging with history. But they were about to expand their culinary repertoire more than they could have possibly imagined. Picture a skilled cook discovering for the first time tomatoes, potatoes, peppers, chocolate, corn, coffee, avocados, vanilla, squash, and beans. Try to imagine European cooking without some of these "new" foods. The native people of the Americas taught the Spaniards how to use these ingredients, and the result is eclectic regional Latin American cuisine that spreads from California to the tip of Chile.

*Clockwise, from left:*
*Patio dining, with mural by Sergio Moyano. The El Farol kitchen*
*serves six to seven hundred tapas nightly.*

Here in Santa Fe we have access to a variety of Latin American foods, and we are fond of the lively spices that touch the soul of the local Pueblo Indian–influenced cuisine. On top of all this, El Farol chefs of various cultural backgrounds have added dashes and pinches of themselves to the mix over the years. My own roots include Italian, Basque, and Irish, and our current staff represents Mexico, El Salvador, Guatemala, Argentina, Uruguay, Poland, and New Mexico.

We love to share these recipes with you and hope this style of cooking will inspire you to experiment as you incorporate some new ideas into your everyday cooking.

—CHEF JAMES

*Buen Provecho!*

# Acknowledgments

Muchas gracias to the people of Santa Fe for their loyal support over the years; David and Karen Salazar and family; Debbie Montoya and family; Genovevo Rivera; Alvaro Ramirez; Los Cocineros! (gracias); the El Farol staff, past and present; the National Institute of Flamenco; the Santa Fe Restaurant Association; Santa Fe Wine and Chile Fiesta; Santa Fe School of Cooking; the Spanish Table; Happy Quail Farms; Spanish Colonial Arts Society; all of the dancers, singers, and musicians who have graced our stages; and Butch Crouch. To the artists the late Alfred Morang, Roland Van Loon, Sergio Moyano, Stan Natchez, and William Vincent. And to Gene Gonzales; Antoinette (Caruso) Campbell; Frances Caruso; and Leslie, Emma, and Liam Campbell.

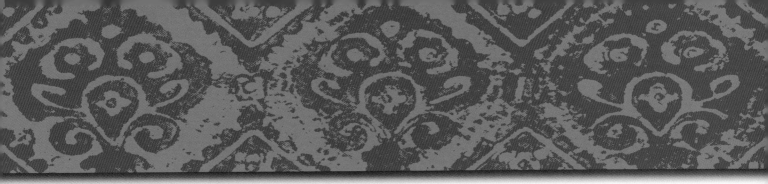

# El Farol
# Basics

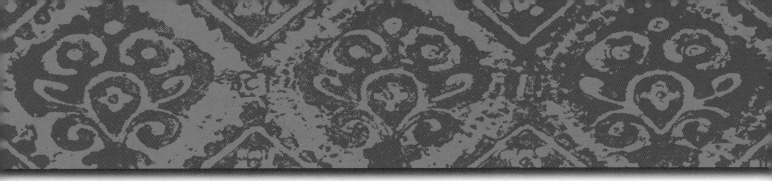

# Sofrito
## Tomato and Garlic Base

*Sofrito is a basic building block in Spanish cooking. Try keeping some on hand as a starter for stews, soups, sauces, and paellas.*

MAKES 3 CUPS

2 yellow onions, peeled and diced
2 red bell peppers, diced
$^1/_2$ cup olive oil
6 roma tomatoes, peeled and diced
6 cloves garlic, minced
2 tablespoons sherry vinegar
1 poblano chile, diced
1 tablespoon paprika
small pinch saffron
$^1/_4$ cup diced jamon serrano (optional)

Sauté onions and peppers in olive oil until very soft and sweet, about 20 minutes. Add the tomatoes and garlic and cook for another 20 minutes. Deglaze the pan with sherry vinegar and stir in all other ingredients; cook for 10 minutes. Sofrito will keep in the refrigerator, covered, for up to 1 week.

# Basic Aioli

*Hand-Mixed Garlic Mayonnaise*

*Here is a basic recipe for the famous sauce that can be slathered on almost anything. We like to keep this very traditional and hand-blend it with a mortar and pestle. There is some question as to whether aioli originated in Italy, France, or Spain. I won't get into the debate, but will say that these great olive oil cultures probably instinctively mixed in some garlic simultaneously. In Spain there are many different spellings: aioli, alioli, allioli, ali-oli.*

MAKES 1 1/4 CUPS

6 cloves garlic
juice of 1 lemon
2 egg yolks
1 teaspoon sea salt
1 cup extra virgin olive oil

Smash the garlic with a mortar and pestle, then add the lemon juice, egg yolks, and sea salt. Stir into a thick paste. Continue to stir while slowly adding the olive oil. Keep stirring until it reaches an even, thick consistency. Adjust seasoning to taste. The aioli should be fairly thick, but if you would like to thin it down, stir in a little water, a teaspoon at a time.

# Lemon-Caper Aioli
## Lemon-Caper Mayonnaise

*Here is a fast mayonnaise version that we like on sausages and grilled salmon; try it also with fried calamari.*

MAKES 2 CUPS

1³/₄ cups mayonnaise
2 tablespoons capers
1 tablespoon pickling liquid from the jar of capers
2 tablespoons Dijon mustard
cracked black pepper
juice of 1 lemon
¹/₂ white onion, diced

Put all ingredients in a food processor and blend well. Lemon-Caper Aioli keeps for up to 2 weeks in the refrigerator, when kept in a jar with a tight lid. ❧

# Aioli de Higos

*Ginger Fig Puree*

We like to use this sweet and savory paste with chutney-like flavor combinations on sliced smoked duck, ham, or grilled lamb.

$^1/_2$ white onion, diced

$^1/_4$ cup olive oil

4 cloves garlic, chopped

1-inch piece of fresh ginger, peeled and chopped

$^1/_4$ cup oloroso sherry

juice of 1 orange

zest of 1 orange

$1^1/_2$ cups chopped dried figs

2 tablespoons hearty mustard

$^1/_4$ cup honey

salt to taste

Sauté the onion in the olive oil until soft. Add the garlic and ginger and sauté for 1 more minute. Deglaze the pan with sherry and orange juice. Transfer to a food processor and combine with all other ingredients except salt. Season to taste with salt. Aioli de Higos can be kept in the refrigerator for up to 3 weeks in a jar with a tight lid.  ❧

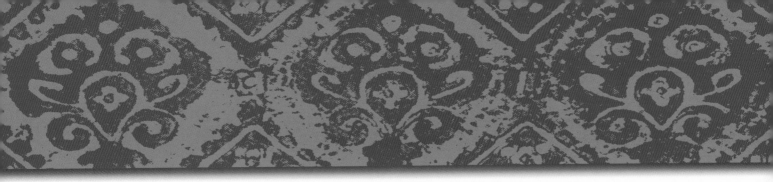

# Aioli de Garbanzos

*Garlic Chickpea Mayonnaise*

*This aioli is a great complement
to grilled salmon and shrimp.
You can also spread it on grilled
breads and serve with seafood stews.*

MAKES 2 CUPS

2 egg yolks
1 tablespoon minced garlic
1 tablespoon fresh lemon juice
$^1/_2$ cup cooked garbanzo beans
2 teaspoons sherry vinegar
pinch of sea salt
$1^1/_2$ cups extra virgin olive oil

Put egg yolks, garlic, lemon juice, garbanzos, and vinegar in the bowl of a food
processor. Blend well for 30 seconds. Add salt. Pour olive oil in while the motor
is still running; add slowly in a fine, steady stream until the mixture thickens
and emulsifies. Transfer to bowl and refrigerate. Aioli de Garbanzo keeps for
2 to 3 days, covered, in the refrigerator. ❧

# Green Onion Butter

*Green Onion Butter's springy fresh taste goes well with fish. We serve it with grilled salmon or add it to steamed clams.*

MAKES 2 CUPS

1 cup butter
$^1/_2$ bunch green onions, chopped
$^1/_2$ cup heavy cream
2 cloves garlic
3 tablespoons white wine
2 tablespoons chopped parsley
salt and pepper to taste

Put all ingredients in a food processor and mix well. Chill and spoon over hot grilled fish. ❧

# Pesto Moro

*Moroccan Olive Pesto*

*Here is another condiment with
North African spice and spirit.
Use this olive paste on grilled
bread, seafood, or with
empanadas.*

MAKES ABOUT 2 CUPS

1 cup pitted Moroccan salt-cured black olives

$^3/_4$ cup extra virgin olive oil

1 teaspoon hot smoked paprika

1 teaspoon ground coriander seed

$^1/_2$ cup chopped fresh parsley

$^1/_2$ cup chopped fresh mint

1 tablespoon minced garlic

Blend all ingredients well with mortar and pestle or in a food processor.
Moroccan Olive Pesto will keep in the refrigerator for 2 to 3 weeks in a jar with a
tight lid.  ﾻ

# Cabrales Butter

*This butter can be used as a spread on warm bread or stirred into cooked vegetables. Our favorite way to eat this unique, pungent blue cheese is with beef.*

MAKES 2 CUPS

1 cup butter
1 cup crumbled Cabrales cheese
2 tablespoons white wine
1 teaspoon cracked black pepper

Combine all ingredients well in a food processor. Keep cold until ready to use.

To use with beef, slowly melt the butter a few tablespoons at a time over low heat while swirling in the pan. Pour over sliced beef. ❧

# El Farol Preserved Lemons

*This is an ancient Mediterranean craft of preserving lemons that can be used in a variety of interesting ways in Spanish cooking. The lemons add a tangy, briny flavor to sauces and roasted fish or chicken. A little goes a long way because this curing process seriously concentrates and deepens the lemon flavor. The process takes about 2 weeks and then the lemons can be rinsed, chopped, and kept packed in oil for 6 months to a year. You will need a clean quart-size glass jar with a tight lid.*

MAKES 1 QUART

6 to 8 lemons
2 cups sea salt
1 stick of cinnamon or Mexican canela
1 teaspoon whole cloves
6 cloves garlic, peeled
2 tablespoons olive oil

Cut lemons in half. Squeeze the juice from half of the lemons and reserve. Put a 1-inch layer of sea salt in the bottom of a quart-size glass jar. Toss all the lemon pieces with remaining sea salt, cinnamon, cloves, and garlic. Firmly pack mixture into the jar and then cover with lemon juice. Top with olive oil. Cover jar tightly and leave at room temperature for 2 to 3 weeks.

When ready, most of the fleshy fruit part of the lemon will have been broken down and eaten away by the salt. Rinse lemon pieces; scrape out any remaining pulp and discard. The preserved rinds can now be used for cooking, or they can be packed in olive oil for future use. I like to chop them in $1/_8$-inch pieces before packing them in oil. This makes using a small spoonful in a recipe very simple.

# Preserved Lemon Butter Sauce

*I like to serve this sauce over small pieces of poached salmon with crispy fried grape leaves for a balanced rich and tangy summer tapa. It is a classic European-style butter emulsion that can be created by swirling butter in your sauce until it finds the right balance of acid and fat.*

MAKES 1$^1/_2$ CUPS

$^1/_4$ cup white wine
1 tablespoon sherry vinegar
1 tablespoon chopped preserved lemons
$^3/_4$ cup butter, cut into $^1/_2$-inch cubes
1 teaspoon honey
dash of salt

Heat the wine and vinegar in a small saucepan on high heat until reduced by half. Turn the heat down to low and add the preserved lemons. Swirl the sauté pan over the low heat with one hand while adding butter, 2 to 3 pieces at a time, with the other hand. Keep swirling until you have melted all of the butter into the sauce. The sauce should be holding together in a nice glossy emulsion. Swirl in the honey and salt. Serve immediately.  ❧

# Green Olive Vinaigrette

*This tangy puree goes great with beef empanadas, grilled fish, or vegetables.*

MAKES ABOUT 2 CUPS

1 cup green olives, pitted
$^1/_4$ cup cornichons (specialty pickles)
2 tablespoons cornichon juice
$^1/_4$ cup chopped parsley
$^1/_2$ tablespoon minced garlic
salt and pepper to taste
1 cup extra virgin olive oil

Blend all ingredients except oil in food processor. Pour in oil while motor is running. Strain well into a jar. Adjust seasoning to taste. Vinaigrette will keep for 7 to 10 days. ⌒

# Saffron Vinaigrette

*This is a versatile sauce for roasted vegetables, salads, or grilled fish.*

MAKES 2 CUPS

1 yellow onion, diced
1 cup extra virgin olive oil
$1/_4$ teaspoon saffron threads
2 cloves garlic
$1/_4$ cup fruity white wine
$1/_4$ cup apple cider vinegar
juice of 1 lemon
$1/_4$ teaspoon ground white pepper
$1/_4$ teaspoon salt

Sauté the onion in a few tablespoons of olive oil for 2 minutes on medium heat. Add saffron and garlic; sauté for 1 minute more. Add white wine and cook until almost all the liquid has been reduced. Remove from heat and transfer to a food processor. Add all other ingredients except the remaining oil. Start the motor and, while running, add the oil in a slow, steady stream until emulsified. It will keep 4 to 5 days in the refrigerator. ❧

# Chipotle-Mustard Vinaigrette

*I originally created this for a spinach and bacon salad, but it has become a very versatile dressing for grilled meats, seafood, and salads. It is based on a classic honey-mustard dressing, but the flavor is deepened and injected with the smoky heat of the Mexican chipotle chile.*

MAKES 2 CUPS

2 cans chipotle chiles en adobo (or more if you like it hot)

$^1/_2$ cup balsamic vinegar

$^1/_2$ cup honey

2 tablespoons Dijon mustard

1 tablespoon minced fresh garlic

salt to taste

$1^1/_2$ cups olive oil

Puree the chiles and put in a mixing bowl. Add all remaining ingredients except oil and whisk together. While whisking, add olive oil in a slow, steady stream until the dressing comes together and emulsifies. Store in the refrigerator for up to 1 week in a glass container. ∾

# Vinagre de Jerez
### Sherry Vinegar Reduction

*This is excellent on tomatoes, salads, and grilled vegetables.*

MAKES 1¹/₂ CUPS

2¹/₂ cups sherry vinegar
1 tomato, diced
¹/₂ red bell pepper, diced
2 cloves garlic, whole
2 tablespoons honey

Combine all ingredients except honey in a saucepan. Bring to a boil and then turn down to simmer. Simmer on medium heat for about 7 minutes. Strain and stir in the honey. Keep refrigerated for 2 to 3 weeks in a glass container.

# Mojo Verde
*Cilantro Paste*

*A tangy condiment to top grilled seafood or meat. Try stirring this into soups at the last minute; the flavor is better if it is not cooked very much.*

MAKES $1^1/_2$ CUPS

1 large bunch fresh cilantro, stems removed (about 2 cups)
$^1/_4$ cup lemon juice
$^1/_2$ cup olive oil
$^1/_2$ teaspoon ground cumin
salt

Thoroughly clean the cilantro and chop it in a food processor. While it is processing, gradually add the remaining ingredients until the mixture is a deep green, aromatic puree. Store in a glass jar with a tight lid. It will keep for 7 to 10 days in the refrigerator. ꙮ

# Pickled Red Onions

*Pickled Red Onions are one of our favorite condiments at El Farol because they are easy to make, keep well in the refrigerator, and add a flashy color to dishes. And they taste great!*

MAKES ABOUT 2 CUPS

1 bay leaf

1 tablespoon coriander, toasted

1 jalapeño or serrano chile

1 tablespoon black peppercorns

$1^1/_2$ cups red wine vinegar

1 cup water

1 tablespoon salt

2 red onions, julienned

2 tablespoons brown sugar

Put all ingredients except onions and sugar in a saucepan; bring to a boil. Add onions and return to boil for 30 seconds. Remove from heat and stir in the sugar. Set aside to cool to room temperature for about an hour. Store in a glass jar and refrigerate for 2 to 3 weeks. ∾

# Compota de Manzanas y Vino

Red Wine–Apple Compote

*Fall means luscious apples in northern New Mexico from Velarde and Dixon. This recipe appears on the El Farol menu with grilled venison or lamb.*

MAKES 2 CUPS

2 cups diced Granny Smith apples
1 red onion, diced
1 tablespoon minced garlic
2 tablespoons butter
1 cup red wine
$^1/_2$ cup brown sugar
pinch of salt
1 tablespoon finely chopped fresh rosemary

Sauté apples, onion, and garlic in butter until soft, stirring frequently. Add red wine, sugar, salt, and rosemary, and cook on high heat for about 5 to 7 minutes. Cool to room temperature and serve with grilled meats. ❧

# Moroccan Carrot Sauce

*Sweet and savory flavors of Morocco are an important aspect of Spanish cuisine. They satisfy our hunger in Santa Fe for exotic flavor combinations. We serve this sauce with roasted duck breast, chicken, and quail.*

MAKES 8 CUPS

1 yellow onion, diced
2 teaspoons minced garlic
3 teaspoons ground cumin
2 teaspoons ground coriander
2 teaspoons ground cinnamon
10 carrots, peeled and chopped
8 cups Chicken Stock (page 37)
1 can orange juice concentrate
2 tablespoons honey
2 teaspoons chile pequin (crushed red pepper)
salt and pepper

Sauté onion and garlic in a skillet. Add spices and carrots. Stir. Add remaining ingredients and boil until carrots are soft. Puree in a blender and strain through a wire mesh. Adjust seasoning to taste.  ❧

# Espresso-Chipotle Sauce

*This is a favorite of mine; it is a contemporary infusion sauce with bold flavor. We serve Espresso-Chipotle Sauce with grilled quail, and it has become a very popular El Farol standard.*

MAKES 4 CUPS

$1^1/_2$ cups espresso beans

1 cup white wine

8 cups Chicken Stock (page 37)

2 roma tomatoes

2 cups tomato juice

1 stick of canela or cinnamon

1 tablespoon coriander seed, toasted and ground

$^1/_4$ cup chipotle puree

$^1/_4$ cup brown sugar

$^1/_4$ cup molasses

salt and pepper to taste

Toast the espresso beans in the bottom of a dry saucepan on medium heat until the coffee aroma develops and the beans start to look oily. Add all ingredients into the saucepan and bring to a boil. Reduce to simmer and continue simmering until the sauce is reduced by half. Strain. Adjust seasoning to taste.

# Aji Amarillo Salsa

*Chile Salsa*

We make this for the staff when
we all need a good chile fix. Our
new favorite chile is the aji amarillo from South America. It is a
burnt orange–yellow color. You
can substitute fresh habaneros or
good, spicy jalapeños.

MAKES 2 CUPS

3 to 4 aji amarillo pods, stems removed

2 cups warm water for soaking the chiles

2 tablespoons roasted peanut oil

$^1/_2$ yellow onion, diced

4 cloves garlic, minced

2 roma or yellow plum tomatoes, diced

2 cups additional water for the sauce

2 teaspoons lime juice

salt to taste

Soak chiles in warm water for 45 minutes and then discard the water. *(Note: Fresh chiles do not need to be soaked.)* Pour peanut oil into a small saucepan and set on high heat. Sauté the onion until soft, then add garlic. Add the tomatoes and sauté for 1 minute. Add the water, lime juice, and chiles. Bring to a boil; reduce heat and simmer for about 10 minutes. Transfer mixture to a food processor and puree. Adjust seasoning with salt. You can thin the salsa with a little water if it is too thick. ❧

# Harissa Sauce

*Moroccan Spiced Chile Sauce*

*If ever a sauce could "float like a butterfly and sting like a bee," this is it. It's a classic, thick, Moroccan spiced chile sauce that our local "chileheads" can relate to because of the heat. But underneath is an exotic, flavorful North African spice blend that gives this condiment its elevated status. Use it on roasted chicken, grilled fish and shrimp, and pork. It adds punch to just about anything and keeps very well in the refrigerator.*

MAKES 2 CUPS

1 red bell pepper, roasted and peeled

2 roma tomatoes, roasted until skin is blackened

1 teaspoon whole cloves

1 tablespoon whole fennel seeds

1 teaspoon whole cumin seeds

6 cloves garlic

2 tablespoons hot smoked paprika

2 tablespoons crushed red chile flakes

3 tablespoons ground New Mexico red chile

juice of 1 orange

2 tablespoons sherry vinegar

2 tablespoons canned tomato puree

1 tablespoon tomato paste

$1/4$ cup water

1 teaspoon salt

1 teaspoon black pepper

The best way to bring out the earthy sweet flavor of bell peppers and tomatoes is to char the skins over an open flame, on a gas or charcoal grill, or in an oven broiler until the peppers and tomatoes are blackened on all sides; remove most of the skin and seeds from the peppers, but leave the tomatoes as they are.

For any of these methods the tomatoes can cool to room temperature or be used right away. Place the peppers in a plastic bag and allow to sweat for 10 to 12 minutes; the skin will soften and be easy to peel. To peel the skins of the peppers, rub with a slightly damp kitchen towel. Do not run water over the peppers because you will dilute that nice rustic charred flavor.

Heat a sauté pan and add the cloves and fennel seeds. Toast while tossing in the pan until smoking hot but not burnt (about 40 seconds). Remove from heat and add the cumin seeds; the residual heat from the pan and the other spices will be enough to toast the cumin. Grind this spice mixture with a mortar and pestle or in an electric coffee grinder and set aside.

In a food processor, puree the bell pepper, tomatoes, and garlic into a fine paste; add all other ingredients and blend well. The harissa should be a fairly thick paste; you can thin it with a little water if you like. Store in a covered container in the refrigerator for up to 1 month. ∾

# Port-Fig Syrup

*This is a very simple and versatile sauce that we serve with roasted pork. You can also use it over ice cream or tossed with fresh fruit.*

4 cups port wine
$1^1/_2$ cups chopped dried figs
pinch of salt

Mix all ingredients in a saucepan and bring to a boil. Turn down to medium heat and simmer until it is reduced by about half. Allow to cool to room temperature. Strain through a wire mesh strainer and chill. It will keep for 2 weeks in the refrigerator. ❧

# Toasted Cumin Tomato Sauce

*The rich, seedy-nutty flavor of cumin is pushed forward by toasting whole seeds. We like this sauce with roasted chicken as well as seared tuna.*

MAKES $2^1/_2$ CUPS

1 tablespoon whole cumin seed
$^1/_2$ white onion, diced
$^1/_4$ cup good olive oil
$^1/_4$ cup sweet cooking sherry
6 roma tomatoes, diced
6 cloves garlic
1 cup tomato juice
salt and black pepper

Toast cumin seeds in a hot, dry skillet by tossing the seeds for about 1 minute over high heat. Grind in mortar and pestle, or any kind of spice grinder, and set aside. In a small saucepan on high heat, sauté onion in olive oil until soft. Add sherry and cook for 2 minutes. Then add tomatoes, garlic, tomato juice, and cumin; turn heat down to medium and cook for 5 more minutes. Puree very well in a blender.  ◐

# Pernod Saffron Cream Sauce

*We like this licoricy cream with halibut, sea bass, or steamed clams.*

MAKES 4 CUPS

1 yellow onion, diced
1 stalk of celery, diced
2 tablespoons butter
1 bay leaf
$^1/_2$ cup Pernod
1 teaspoon saffron
2 cups heavy cream
$1^1/_2$ cups Fish Stock (page 39)
juice of $^1/_2$ lemon
salt and white pepper to taste

Sauté the onion and celery in butter until soft but not browned. Add the bay leaf, Pernod, and saffron. Simmer for 5 minutes. Add the cream and Fish Stock and simmer for 10 to 15 minutes more until partially reduced. Add the lemon juice and remove from heat. Strain and season with salt and white pepper to taste. Pernod Saffron Cream Sauce keeps in the refrigerator for 2 to 3 days. Reheat slowly for use. ❧

# Mediterranean Salsa

*Mediterranean salsa is excellent served with grilled bread.*

6 tomatoes, diced

2 tablespoons capers

1 cup kalamata olives, pitted and cut in half

1 tablespoon minced garlic

$1/_2$ red onion, diced fine

2 tablespoons chopped parsley

3 tablespoons balsamic vinegar

$1/_4$ cup extra virgin olive oil

salt and pepper to taste

Mix all ingredients together well in a bowl and let stand at room temperature. ◦◦

# Romesco Sauce

*Almond, Garlic, Red Pepper Sauce*

*This is an extremely versatile classic condiment of Spanish descent, and you will end up using it on everything! We have a few customers who order a small bowl of this with some bread as a tapa. A few of our favorite uses are with Patatas Bravas (page 129), Tortilla Española (page 79), El Farol Fried Calamari (page 114), and empanadas (pages 91, 94, 96, and 98).*

MAKES ABOUT 4 CUPS

1 cup Marcona almonds, toasted
10 cloves garlic
1 cup extra virgin olive oil
2 tablespoons sherry vinegar
2 to 3 dried piquin chilies
2 cups charred, peeled, and chopped roasted red bell peppers
salt

Char the red bell peppers over an open flame, on a gas or charcoal grill, or in an over broiler until the peppers are blackened on all sides. Remove most of the skin and seeds from the peppers.

In a blender or food processor, puree the almonds, garlic, oil, vinegar, and chiles until smooth. Add peppers, replace the top, and pulse until the sauce is just a bit chunky. Salt to taste. This sauce will keep for 4 to 5 days if refrigerated.

Romesco Sauce

# Curry Oil

*This is a key ingredient in our famous curried chicken salad, but I like to have it on hand to drizzle on other foods such as grilled fish, mashed potatoes, rice dishes, or just on bread.*

MAKES 1 CUP

1 tablespoon whole coriander seeds
1 tablespoon whole mustard seeds
1 teaspoon whole cloves
1 tablespoon whole cumin seeds
1 teaspoon ground turmeric
2 tablespoons curry powder
1 teaspoon smoked hot paprika
1 tablespoon cayenne pepper
zest of 1 lime
zest of 1 lemon
1 cup olive oil

Toast coriander, mustard seeds, and cloves on high heat in a dry pan until spices are smoking. Remove from heat and add cumin seeds. Toss spices together in the hot pan, then add remaining ingredients except oil.

In a separate, small saucepan, heat the oil to about 250 degrees. Remove from heat and stir in spice mixture. Let the oil sit to infuse with spices for at least 1 hour at room temperature. Strain through a fine sieve lined with paper. Store for 2 to 3 weeks in the refrigerator. ∽

# Paprika Oil

This intensely colored, flavored oil adds depth to many dishes. It can be served with bread for dipping, or drizzled on grilled vegetables and fish. We use a spicy, smoked paprika from Spain. Sometimes we add some punch with other ground chiles, such as cayenne, and change the name to Sangre del Diablo (Devil's Blood).

MAKES ABOUT 2 CUPS

2 cups olive oil
$1/4$ cup paprika
1 tablespoon salt
4 cloves garlic, minced

Heat oil in a saucepan until warm. Stir in paprika, salt, and garlic. Let stand for 30 minutes, then strain through a fine sieve. Store in the refrigerator for 2 to 3 weeks. ❧

# Migas
## Fried Bread

A simple use for leftover bread is to make these crispy garlic croutons. They are great on top of salads and soups, served as a tapa with aioli, or mixed with chunks of fried chorizo. We also like to serve these as a staff meal topped with fried eggs. Keep some migas on hand in an airtight container and crush them into stews, soups, and sauces as a rustic, flavorful thickener.

MAKES 2 CUPS

1 tablespoon chopped fresh parsley
1 teaspoon kosher salt
$^{1}/_{2}$ teaspoon cracked black pepper
$^{1}/_{2}$ cup paprika oil
4 cloves garlic, peeled and thinly sliced
4 thick slices rustic white bread or baguette, cut into 1-inch cubes

Mix parsley, salt, and pepper in a bowl and set aside. Heat the oil in a skillet to a high temperature and add the garlic. Cook until browned and crispy, about $1^{1}/_{2}$ minutes. Remove with a slotted spoon and add to parsley mixture.

Fry the bread cubes in the hot oil, stirring to fry all sides, until golden and slightly crispy, about 5 minutes. Remove from the oil and transfer to a bowl; toss with the garlic, parsley, salt, and pepper mixture.

# Salsa Verde with Fennel Seed

*This versatile condiment can be used as is on grilled meats or seafood to add a lively green flavor. Also try mixing some into cooked rice or soup.*

MAKES ABOUT 1 CUP

2 tablespoons fennel seeds
2 cloves garlic
juice of $1/_2$ lime
$1/_4$ cup chopped parsley
$1/_4$ cup chopped mint
$1/_4$ cup extra virgin olive oil

Crush fennel seeds with mortar and pestle. Add garlic and lime juice, and crush into a fine paste. Add parsley, mint, and olive oil. Continue to crush until a thick, spoonable sauce is achieved. Keeps for 3 to 4 days if refrigerated.

# El Farol Pincho Spice Mix

*Pinchos are grilled skewered meat kebobs. Pinchos Morunos are the famous Moorish-style pork or lamb version with an exotic blend of North African spices. This spice mixture is our unique blend that can be kept on hand to rub on almost anything that's grilled! We've used it with lamb, pork, chicken, rabbit, mushrooms, shrimp, and beef.*

*Hint: Don't make too much El Farol Pincho Spice Mix at a time. The process of buying your spices whole, toasting them, and grinding them yourself is designed to maximize the flavor. Once a spice is ground, the essence of the flavor begins dissipating into the air.*

MAKES ABOUT $^1/_2$ CUP

1 tablespoon coriander seeds
1 tablespoon cumin seeds
1 tablespoon fennel seeds
1 teaspoon star anise
1 teaspoon whole cloves
1 dry chipotle chile
1 teaspoon sea salt
1 teaspoon sweet smoked paprika
1 teaspoon dried Mexican oregano
1 bay leaf
1 pinch of saffron
4 cloves garlic
3 tablespoons olive oil
1 tablespoon fresh lemon juice

Toast the whole spices (coriander, cumin, fennel, star anise, cloves, and chipotle chile) in a hot, dry pan until smoking. Crush in a mortar and pestle, then add all other dry spices and mix well. At this point the mixture can be stored with a tight cover for about 1 week. When it's time to grill, crush the garlic with the oil and lemon juice and form a paste. Mix with the dry mixture, rub the paste into your meat, and let it marinate for 2 to 3 hours before grilling. ❧

# Chicken Stock

*We keep this handy to use as a flavorful base for many dishes and soups.*

MAKES 1 GALLON

1 lemon
1 whole chicken (3 to 4 pounds)
salt and pepper
2 stalks of celery
1 yellow onion, peeled and halved
2 carrots
2 gallons water
1 tablespoon black peppercorns
1 tablespoon fennel seeds
2 sticks of canela or cinnamon
2 cups amontillado sherry

Preheat oven to 375 degrees. Perforate the lemon by poking it with a fork many times. Stuff the lemon into the cavity of the chicken. Rub the chicken skin with salt and pepper. Place the chicken, celery, onion, and carrots on a sheet pan and roast for 45 minutes. Transfer chicken and vegetables to a large stockpot and add the remaining ingredients. Bring to a boil, then turn down heat and simmer for 1 hour. Strain and use as a cooking liquid. ❧

# Jamon Stock

*A hearty ham stock to use in soups and sauces, and for cooking rice.*

MAKES 1 GALLON

1 pound ham bones or hocks
1 yellow onion, quartered
2 stalks of celery
2 carrots, peeled
2 gallons of water
$^1/_4$ cup olive oil
1 potato, quartered
6 cloves garlic, crushed
1 bay leaf
1 tablespoon black peppercorns
1 stick of canela or cinnamon

Preheat oven to 375 degrees. Place the ham bones, onion, celery, and carrots on a sheet pan and roast for 40 minutes. When finished roasting, place ham bones and vegetables in a large stockpot with the remaining ingredients. Bring to a boil, then turn down to simmer for about 1 hour. Strain and use as a cooking liquid. ❧

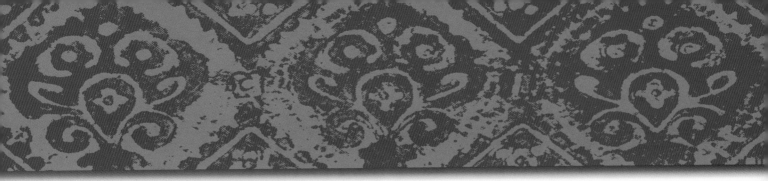

# Fish Stock

*This is a flavorful cooking liquid
for soups, stews, sauces, and paellas.
Make about 2 gallons and freeze it
for future use. Your local fish mar-
ket or grocery should be able to
provide the fish bones and scraps.
Look for mild white fish scraps and
stay away from swordfish, tuna, or
salmon because their flavors are
too strong for the stock.*

MAKES 2 GALLONS

$1^{1}/_{2}$ pounds of fish bones and scraps

1 white onion

2 carrots

2 stalks of celery

1 bulb of fennel

1 head of garlic

$^{1}/_{4}$ cup olive oil

1 tablespoon sea salt

1 tablespoon coriander seeds

$2^{1}/_{2}$ gallons water

3 cups white wine

Preheat oven to 400 degrees. Lay the fish bones, vegetables, and garlic on a sheet
pan, then drizzle with olive oil and sprinkle with salt. Put in the oven and roast for
20 to 30 minutes until the vegetables are lightly browned. This will allow the sweetness of the vegetables to surface and will deepen the flavor of the stock. Transfer to
a stockpot and add all other ingredients. Bring to a boil and then turn down to a
low simmer; simmer for about 1 hour. Strain and use as a cooking liquid. ❧

# Sopas y Caldos

# Fabada

*Asturian White Bean Stew with Chorizo, Blood Sausage, and Ham*

*Fabada is a hearty bean stew for a cold winter night, or a rich, one-pot meal that can feed the family for a few days. Try experimenting with different beans as well as substituting your favorite sausages. Don't be afraid to make your own memorable family version.*

MAKES 10 SERVINGS

1 pound dried Great Northern white beans
2 smoked ham hocks
1 ham bone
2 bay leaves
1 tablespoon smoked hot paprika
6 quarts water
1/4 cup olive oil
6 cloves garlic, chopped
1 pound good Spanish chorizo, sliced
1/2 pound morcilla (blood sausage), sliced
2 roma tomatoes, diced

Cover the beans in a bowl with cold water to rinse, and let them soak for a few hours. In a stockpot, put ham hocks and ham bone covered with water; bring to a boil. Turn down heat and simmer for 30 minutes. Remove hocks and bone from stock and set aside. Drain beans and put them in the pot with the ham stock. Add the bay leaves, paprika, and about 6 quarts of water. Bring to a boil and then turn down to simmer for about 2 1/2 hours. Meanwhile, remove all the meat that you can from the ham hocks and ham bone. Dice the meat and sauté in olive oil. Add garlic, chorizo, morcilla, and tomatoes and sauté for 3 more minutes. Add the contents of the sauté pan, including all the pan fat, to the pot of cooked beans. Simmer for a few more minutes and serve in bowls. ∾

# Caldo Pescado

*Fish Soup*

*This is one of our favorite things to eat after a busy night.*

MAKES 6 SERVINGS

1 pound of new potatoes, diced
½ cup olive oil
1 yellow onion, diced
small pinch of saffron
½ cup white wine
1 pound fresh clams
½ pound black mussels
1 roma tomato, diced
1 tablespoon minced garlic
3 cups Fish Stock (page 39)
1 pound of cod or other white fish
1 teaspoon dried Mexican oregano
salt and pepper to taste

Boil the potatoes until very soft. Drain and set aside. Heat the olive oil in a deep skillet and sauté the onion until soft. Add the saffron and white wine. Cook on medium heat for 5 minutes. Add the clams, mussels, tomato, garlic, and Fish Stock; cook covered until clams and mussels pop open. Add the cod and turn down to a simmer for 5 to 7 minutes. Add the oregano and potatoes and season with salt and pepper. Serve in bowls with bread and a nice bottle of Albarino. ❧

# Marmitako

*Fresh Tuna and Potato Stew with Smoked Paprika*

*A simple, classic combination of fish, potatoes, and onions as a one-pot meal or a hearty starter.*

MAKES 4 SERVINGS

1 cup extra virgin olive oil

2 yellow onions, julienned

10 cloves garlic, peeled

3 slices rustic white bread, cut in
   $^1\!/_2$-inch cubes

2 tablespoons chopped Italian parsley

1 quart Fish Stock (page 39)

6 new potatoes with peel on, cut in
   $^1\!/_4$-inch dice

1 tablespoon sherry vinegar

$^1\!/_2$ cup white wine

1 teaspoon fresh thyme leaves

1 teaspoon chopped fresh oregano

2 teaspoons sweet smoked paprika

2 pounds fresh tuna, cut in
   $^1\!/_2$-inch cubes

Heat $^1\!/_2$ cup of the olive oil on medium heat in a 2-quart saucepan and add the onions. Cook onions slowly, stirring often to prevent sticking. Lower heat if needed. This will caramelize the onions and allow the maximum sweetness to come to the surface. This should take about 30 minutes.

Meanwhile, heat $^1\!/_2$ cup olive oil to moderately high heat in a small saucepan. Add garlic and fry until golden brown, about 5 minutes. Remove garlic with a slotted spoon and set aside. Add bread to hot oil and fry until brown and crispy, about 2 minutes. Remove the bread and set aside.

Crush fried garlic, fried bread, and parsley with a mortar and pestle. Set mixture aside. Bring Fish Stock to a boil and add potatoes. Cook for 10 minutes. Add sherry vinegar, wine, thyme, oregano, and smoked paprika to the caramelized onions and cook for 5 minutes on medium heat. Add tuna and cook for another five minutes. Add Fish Stock with cooked potatoes to the pot. Bring to a boil and stir in bread-garlic mixture. Turn down to simmer for 5 minutes. Serve hot.  ∾

# Oyster-Potato Soup

*So simple, quick, and delicious, this appetizing soup becomes a meal with some good flat bread and a salad.*

MAKES ABOUT 8 SERVINGS

2 tablespoons butter

1 yellow onion, diced

4 cloves garlic, crushed

6 Yukon Gold potatoes, cut in very small dice with peel on

2 cups clam juice

2 cups Chicken Stock (page 37)

2 cups heavy cream

1/2 cup white wine

salt and cracked black pepper to taste

1 1/2 pounds fresh oysters, shucked

Melt butter in saucepan and sauté onion until soft, then add garlic. Add potatoes and sauté for about 2 minutes on high heat. Add all other ingredients except oysters and bring to a boil. Turn down the heat and simmer until potatoes are soft, about 5 minutes. Add oysters, simmer for 2 to 3 minutes more, and serve. ❧

# Posole Clam Chowder

This is a very southwestern version
of New England clam chowder.
Posole *is a Pueblo Indian food. It is
white corn dried in the high
desert sun. You could substitute
canned hominy, as it is very
similar and much easier to find in
most places in the U.S. The smoky
heat of this dish comes from
chipotle chile, a Mexican red
jalapeño that is dried and then
smoked over mesquite. You can find
canned* chipotles en adobo, *a
hydrated form of the chile, in some
supermarkets or Hispanic markets.*

MAKES ABOUT 8 SERVINGS

4 slices of bacon, chopped
3/4 cup butter
2 yellow onions, chopped
1/4 cup flour
3 cups chopped fresh raw clams
2 cups cooked *posole* or hominy
2 chipotle chiles*
6 cups clam juice
6 cups milk
salt and pepper

In large soup pot, cook bacon on medium heat until it gets slightly crispy.
Add 1/2 cup butter and onions and sauté until soft. Stir in the flour. Add clams,
hominy, chipotle chiles, and clam juice and bring to a boil. Turn heat down and
stir in the rest of the butter and the milk. Simmer for 10 to 15 minutes. Adjust
seasoning with salt, pepper, and chipotle.

*You can use more chiles, but start with 2 and add more if you like. They can be
*hot!* You can also try this with fresh jalapeños instead of chipotles.

# Sopa de Guisantes

*Sweet Pea Rosemary Soup*

*We make this pureed soup with a ham bone stock, but chicken or vegetable stock will work fine. You may need to add a little extra salt and pepper though.*

MAKES **8** SERVINGS

1 yellow onion, diced

2 stalks of celery, chopped

2 carrots

1/4 cup olive oil

1 tablespoon minced fresh garlic

2 tablespoons chopped fresh rosemary

1 cup oloroso sherry

6 cups Jamon Stock (page 38) or Chicken Stock (page 37)

1/2 cup butter

16 ounces fresh or frozen sweet peas

1/2 cup heavy cream

2 teaspoons salt

1 teaspoon white pepper

paprika oil (optional)

jamon serrano, chopped (optional)

In a soup pot, sauté the onion, celery, and carrots in olive oil until soft. Add the garlic and rosemary and sauté for another minute. Add the sherry and cook on medium heat for a few minutes. Add the stock and bring to a boil. Simmer on medium heat for about 15 minutes. Remove from heat, add all other ingredients, and puree well in a blender. Return to the stove and cook for another 5 to 7 minutes at medium heat. Adjust seasoning. Serve hot in bowls and drizzle with paprika oil and some chopped jamon serrano. ◕

Gazpacho

# Gazpacho
*Chilled Raw Tomato Soup*

*This is a classic soup of southern Spain.*

MAKES 8 SERVINGS

10 roma tomatoes, cut in half with stem ends removed
1 red onion, chopped
1 red bell pepper, chopped
2 small cucumbers, peeled, seeded, and chopped
3 slices of rustic white bread, crusts removed
1½ quarts cold water
¼ cup sherry vinegar
1 cup extra virgin olive oil
3 cloves garlic
salt and black pepper to taste
hard-boiled eggs, chopped (optional)

Put all ingredients in a glass or plastic container and allow to stand for 15 minutes. Puree well in a blender and refrigerate for 1 hour. Serve in chilled bowls and top with chopped hard-boiled egg if you like. ∾

# Sopa de Almendras

### Chilled Almond Garlic Soup

*This is a rich, nutty soup enhanced by amontillado sherry for a true taste of southern Spain. For the best result, use whole almonds, preferably Marcona almonds from Spain.*

MAKES 8 SERVINGS

2 thick slices of rustic white bread
1/2 gallon cold water
6 cups whole Marcona almonds
6 cloves garlic
2 teaspoons salt
1 teaspoon cracked black pepper
juice of 1/2 lemon
1/2 cup amontillado sherry

Soak bread in the water. Puree almonds and garlic in food processor. Add the bread-and-water mixture to the food processor and puree well. Add all other ingredients. Strain through a medium-mesh strainer, pushing the almond pulp through with a small ladle. Chill soup for at least 1 hour. Serve in chilled bowls with a glass of amontillado on a warm summer evening.

# Tapas Frias

# Betabeles

*Roasted Beets with Goat Cheese Dressing*

Roasting brings out the earthy
sweetness of the beets. The color
contrast of the deep purple vegetable
and the bright white of the dressing
makes for a nice presentation. Serve
this dish at room temperature.

MAKES 4 TAPA SERVINGS

1 pound fresh beets (red or gold)

$^1/_2$ cup sherry vinegar

$^1/_4$ cup good olive oil

4 cloves garlic, peeled and sliced very thin

1 teaspoon kosher salt

1 teaspoon cracked black pepper

$^1/_2$ teaspoon ground white pepper

Preheat oven to 425 degrees. Wash beets well and trim greens (save the greens; they are excellent for steaming or braising). Cut beets in quarter wedges. Do not peel. Toss with all other ingredients in a large bowl. Transfer to a baking dish and cover with foil. Bake for 35 minutes. Allow to cool to room temperature. Transfer to a platter and spoon the Goat Cheese Dressing (page 61) over the top. ❧

Sandia con Jamon

# Sandia con Jamon

*Watermelon Wrapped in Jamon Serrano*

*A classic melon-and-ham flavor combination with a thick Spanish accent. When the weather is hot, this makes a great snack or starter course.*

MAKES 6 TAPA SERVINGS

6 small triangles of watermelon
6 thin slices of jamon serrano, enough to wrap around each melon piece
1/4 cup extra virgin olive oil
1/2 cup crumbled aged goat cheese, feta cheese, or queso fresco
2 tablespoons chopped fresh mint
1 teaspoon crushed red chile flakes

Wrap each piece of melon with a piece of jamon serrano. Place each wrapped melon piece on a chilled plate and drizzle with olive oil. Sprinkle with cheese, chopped mint, and chile flakes. ❧

# Mejillones al Vinagreta

Chilled Black Mussels in Vinaigrette

This can stand alone as a cold tapa. For a larger salad course, toss with crisp romaine, olive oil, and migas. Serve with lemon wedges.

MAKES 6 TAPA SERVINGS

3 pounds fresh black mussels
1/2 cup white wine
1 cup water
1 red onion, diced
4 green onions, chopped
1 tablespoon Dijon mustard
1/2 cup chopped cornichons (specialty pickles)
1/4 cup of cornichons pickling juice
1 teaspoon minced garlic
2 teaspoons sherry vinegar
1/2 cup extra virgin olive oil
1 bay leaf
sea salt to taste

Steam mussels in white wine and 1 cup of water until opened. Pull each mussel from its shell and toss with all other ingredients. Chill for several hours and serve as a cold tapa. ❧

# Mojama
### Cured Tuna Loin

I am always searching for new ways to serve tuna because it is such a versatile fish and is always a popular menu item. After reading about this cured fish and its likely Phoenician origins, I had to try it. It was one of the first foods I sampled while traveling in southern Spain. In southern coastal towns, they coat the tuna loin in salt and then hang it to wind-cure in the salty breeze. The final product is firm and can be cut into thin, transparent slices to serve as a tapa. Traditionally it is served drizzled with olive oil and eaten with roasted red bell peppers. This fish is difficult to find in the United States, so I developed my own curing process that comes surprisingly close to the real thing. You will need a perforated pan that fits over another pan to catch the juices, as this curing process chemically pulls all the moisture out of the fish while it is refrigerated.

MAKES ABOUT 20 TAPA SERVINGS, 2 TO 3 THIN SLICES PER PORTION

2 cups turbinado (raw sugar)
2 cups sea salt
1 tablespoon hot smoked Spanish paprika
2 pounds fresh tuna, cut into 6-inch-long, 2-inch-wide pieces

Mix sugar, salt, and paprika in a bowl. Pack mixture all around tuna pieces and place tuna in a perforated dish or pan. Pack any remaining salt mixture on top of fish. Place the perforated pan on top of a solid pan or dish to catch drippings, cover with plastic wrap, and refrigerate for 3 to 4 days. Remove from salt mixture and rinse. Slice thin with a sharp knife and serve as a tapa, drizzled with good extra virgin olive oil. Or serve on top of a green salad. ❧

# Jicama with Lime and Catarina Chile

*A nice summertime tapa from Mexico. Jicama is a crunchy, sweet, and refreshing root vegetable that is eaten raw.*

MAKES 8 SERVINGS

2 pounds jicama
1/4 cup fresh-squeezed lime juice
3 tablespoons ground catarina or cascabel chile
1 tablespoon kosher salt
1 lime, cut into thin wedges
a few sprigs of cilantro

Peel jicama and cut into 3/4-inch batons (like thick french fries). Dip one end of each piece in lime juice. Sprinkle some chile on the wet end and arrange pieces on a small plate. Sprinkle with kosher salt. Garnish with lime wedges and cilantro. ❧

# Goat Cheese Dressing

*Excellent with roasted root vegetables such as beets and parsnips. We also use it on summer salads with cucumber, fresh asparagus, and baby carrots.*

MAKES 2 CUPS

1 cup fresh soft goat cheese
$1/2$ cup milk
1 serrano chile, chopped
$1/4$ cup extra virgin olive oil
2 tablespoons fresh lime juice
2 green onions, chopped
3 cloves garlic, minced
1 teaspoon cracked black pepper

Combine all ingredients in a blender or food processor and puree well. Chill for 1 hour to let the flavors come together. ❧

Ensalada de Uvas con Queso

# Ensalada de Uvas con Queso

*Grape Salad with Fresh Mozzarella*

*A pretty summer salad with a nice combination of sweet and tart flavors.*

MAKES 8 TAPA SERVINGS

1 cup seedless green grapes

1 cup seedless red grapes

1/2 cup small cherry or teardrop-shaped tomatoes

1 cup fresh cilengene (small balls of mozzarella,
    or cut a larger ball into 1-inch cubes)

1 cup pitted Moroccan black olives or kalamatas

2 tablespoons chopped fresh mint

1 tablespoon minced fresh garlic

1 teaspoon grated lemon peel

2 tablespoons sherry vinegar

1/4 cup extra virgin olive oil

salt and pepper to taste

Toss all ingredients well and chill for 1 hour before serving. Can be eaten at room temperature.  ❧

# Ceviche
*Fresh Seafood Dish*

*In ceviche, raw fish is "cooked" without heat through a chemical reaction with an acid such as lime juice. The flavors in this dish cleanse the palate.*

MAKES 6 TO 8 SERVINGS

1/2 cup diced tomato
1/2 cup tomato juice
3 tablespoons olive oil
1 pound bay scallops
1/2 pound small shrimp, peeled and deveined
1/2 pound small squid, body cut into rings, tentacles separated
2 bunches scallions, thinly sliced (about 1 cup)
1 bunch fresh cilantro, finely chopped (about 1 cup)
1 large jalapeño chile, chopped
1 tablespoon salt
2 to 3 cups fresh lime juice

Set aside the tomato, tomato juice, and olive oil.

Place all the remaining ingredients except the lime juice in a nonreactive bowl. Pour the juice over the mixture to cover. Marinate in the refrigerator for 2 hours.

Drain the lime juice and toss the mixture with the tomato, tomato juice, and olive oil. Serve ceviche well chilled. ✑

# Bay Scallop Ceviche
*Fresh Bay Scallop Dish*

*Bay scallops are the perfect size and texture for ceviche and their sweetness offers balance to the acidity of the dressing.*

MAKES 6 TO 8 TAPA SERVINGS

1 pound fresh bay scallops

$1/2$ cup lemon juice

$1/2$ cup lime juice

$1/2$ cup orange juice

1 white onion, finely chopped

1 tablespoon salt

1 ear of sweet corn

1 teaspoon white sugar

2 jalapeño chiles, seeded and diced

$1/4$ pound of jamon serrano, sliced thin and chopped

1 cup clam juice

$1/4$ cup olive oil

2 roma tomatoes, diced

Mix scallops in a glass bowl with lemon juice, lime juice, orange juice, onion, and salt. Toss well and refrigerate for 6 to 8 hours. Preheat oven to 400 degrees. Roast corn in its husk for 15 minutes. Remove from oven and let cool for 10 minutes. Shuck the corn and remove kernels from the cob with a knife. Cool. Mix corn and remaining ingredients into the scallop mixture and return to the refrigerator for 1 hour. Serve chilled in small bowls as a tapa. ❧

# Salmon Ceviche with Sweet Corn Vinaigrette

*Fresh Salmon Dish with Sweet Corn Dressing*

*Vibrant pink and yellow colors make this ceviche a great presentation.*

MAKES 6 TAPA SERVINGS

**For Salmon:**

1¹/₂ pounds salmon

1 cup fresh lime juice

1 white onion, diced

1 tablespoon kosher salt

1 tablespoon toasted ground
   coriander seed

**For Corn Dressing:**

1¹/₂ cups fresh sweet corn, blanched

2 tablespoons sherry vinegar

2 tablespoons fino (pale, dry sherry)

¹/₂ cup olive oil

salt and pepper to taste

**To Serve:**

2 roma tomatoes, diced

2 green onions, chopped

Bibb lettuce

pepita flatbread

Paprika Oil (page 33)

Cut salmon into ¹/₂-inch cubes and toss with lime juice, onion, salt, and coriander in a nonreactive container. Refrigerate for 12 hours or up to 24 hours.

Make the corn dressing in a food processor by adding 1 cup of the corn, vinegar, and fino to the bowl. While the motor is running add the olive oil in a slow, steady stream until the mixture emulsifies. Season to taste with salt and pepper.

Remove salmon from lime juice and discard the juice. Toss salmon with the dressing, tomatoes, green onions, and remaining corn. Serve on Bibb lettuce with pepita flatbread and a drizzle of Paprika Oil. ❧

# Mediterranean Couscous Salad

Couscous is formed by grating a ball of pasta dough into fine tiny pieces. This salad is made with Israeli couscous, which is large, pearl-shaped pasta that is toasted after it is formed and dried. Look for it in any natural grocery or Middle Eastern shop.

MAKES 6 TAPA SERVINGS

2 cups toasted Israeli couscous

1 tomato, diced

$1/2$ red onion, diced

$1/4$ cup black olives, pitted and halved

4 cloves garlic, minced

$1/2$ cup extra virgin olive oil

2 tablespoons chopped pepperoncini or other pickled peppers

2 tablespoons sherry vinegar

3 tablespoons chopped fresh parsley

2 tablespoons chopped fresh mint

salt and pepper to taste

Cook couscous in boiling salted water for about 8 minutes or until soft. Drain and rinse. Toss with all other ingredients and season with salt and pepper. Serve at room temperature as a tapa or side dish. ❧

Marinated Olives

# Marinated Olives

Spain harvests over 250 varieties of olives and is the largest producer of olive oil in the world. Since biblical times, olives have been an important part of the culture and economy of the peninsula. One of the best tasting table olives known to man is the Manzanilla olive. These green olives are tangy and juicy with a soft flesh and are perfect for a casual tapa with a glass of sherry. This marinade can be used with almost any green olives.

MAKES 15 TO 20 TAPA SERVINGS

1 quart of Manzanilla or other fleshy green olives

**For Marinade:**
2 cups extra virgin olive oil
3 sprigs of fresh thyme
2 tablespoons chopped garlic
5 to 6 whole cloves
zest of 1 orange

Drain the brine from the olives and discard. Rinse the olives in water. Mix marinade ingredients together and toss with the olives. Marinate in the refrigerator for at least 12 hours before eating. You can store Marinated Olives in a jar with a lid in the refrigerator for 5 to 6 weeks. Pull olives from the refrigerator at least 1 hour before serving; always serve at room temperature. ❧

# Marinated Peruvian Purple Potatoes

*This works as a cold tapa or side potato salad. Any kind of small new potato will do well. However, the blues give not only a vibrant color but an excellent starchy flavor and texture.*

MAKES 8 SERVINGS

2 pounds purple or blue potatoes, quartered with the skins on
1/2 cup extra virgin olive oil
3 tablespoons sherry vinegar
1/2 red onion, diced fine
4 cloves garlic, minced
2 tablespoons chopped fresh Italian flat-leaf parsley
2 teaspoons or more crushed chile pequin (optional)
salt and black pepper to taste
1/4 cup crumbled queso fresco, feta, or ricotta salata

Boil potatoes in salted water until cooked through but still firm. Drain and rinse with cold water. Toss with olive oil, vinegar, onion, garlic, parsley, and chile pequin. Adjust seasoning with salt and pepper. Let stand at room temperature for about an hour. Spoon queso over top and serve. ◌

# Pollo Curri

*Curried Chicken Salad with Celery and Grapes*

*Here is one from the El Farol recipe archives—a simple cold chicken salad that is too good to ever remove from the menu. The flavor secret is the Curry Oil that is mixed with the mayonnaise. Serve as a cold tapa or as a sandwich.*

MAKES 6 SERVINGS

2 pounds pulled chicken, both light and dark meat

1/2 cup red grapes

2 stalks of celery, diced

1 red onion, diced

1 teaspoon cayenne pepper

2 tablespoons Dijon mustard

1 1/2 cups mayonnaise

1/2 cup Curry Oil (page 32)

salt and black pepper to taste

Mix everything together in a bowl and chill for at least an hour. Serve on bread, in sandwiches, or on lettuce for a cold tapa. ❧

# Preserved Lemon Goat Cheese Spread

*This has a nice, lively Mediterranean balance. Spread on warm bread for a tapa and serve with a cool bottle of Albarino white wine.*

MAKES ABOUT 6 TAPA SERVINGS

1 large head of garlic
¼ cup good extra virgin olive oil
8 ounces soft Spanish goat cheese
1 tablespoon chopped Preserved Lemons (page 12)
1 tablespoon chopped fresh mint
2 tablespoons chopped fresh Italian flat-leaf parsley

Preheat oven to 350 degrees. Cut the top end off the garlic—be sure to cut low enough to expose the tops of the cloves. Drizzle the garlic head with olive oil and roast in a covered ceramic pot (or wrapped in foil) for about 35 minutes. Remove from oven and set aside to cool. Mix all other ingredients in a mixing bowl with a wooden spoon. When garlic is cool enough to handle, squeeze the whole garlic and the roasted cloves should slide into the cheese mixture. If the garlic doesn't easily squeeze out, then it probably needs to cook a little more or you'll have to carefully remove it with a fork and avoid getting any garlic peel in your cheese mixture. Stir in the garlic with the wooden spoon; this will leave everything rustic and chunky (you can puree all the ingredients together if you prefer a smoother product). Refrigerate the mixture for an hour to let the flavors come together, but be sure to let it sit at room temperature for 15 to 20 minutes before serving, as it will spread more easily.

# Queso Fresco

*Cheese and Jamon Serrano Wrapped in Grape Leaves*

*There are many fresh, unpasturized cheeses in Spain that are not available in the United States that work well in this recipe, but fresh mozzarella is a good choice here. The large egg-shaped balls work best. To make this tapa, the cheese is filled with jamon serrano and then wrapped in grape leaves.*

MAKES 4 SERVINGS

2 large egg-shaped balls of fresh mozzarella
4 paper-thin slices of jamon serrano or prosciutto
4 large grape leaves
olive oil for sautéing
1/2 cup garlic-flavored olive oil

Cut each ball of cheese into 4 thick slices for a total of 8 slices. Lay a slice of jamon on 4 of the cheese slices, and then top each with the remaining cheese slices. Wrap each "sandwich" with a grape leaf. Heat a sauté pan to high heat and add a few splashes of olive oil. Sear the wrapped cheeses for about 30 seconds per side, until the grape leaf is a little crisp. Transfer to a platter and drizzle with garlic oil. Serve at room temperature. ◕

Shrimp Escabeche with Black Olives and Mint

# Shrimp Escabeche with Black Olives and Mint
Marinated Shrimp Dish

*This is a quick pickled shrimp dish for a hot day.*

MAKES 8 TAPA SERVINGS

3 cups apple cider vinegar

1 cup water

3 cloves garlic, crushed

2 bay leaves

1 teaspoon whole cloves

juice from 2 oranges

zest from 1 orange

1 tablespoon whole black peppercorns

2 tablespoons whole coriander seeds

2 tablespoons salt

2 tablespoons ancho chile powder

1/2 white onion

1 pound large shrimp, peeled and deveined

1/2 cup sliced black olives, with 1/4 cup of brine

2 red onions, julienned

1/2 cup chopped fresh mint

Put all ingredients except the shrimp, olives, red onions, and mint into a large saucepan and bring the reserved liquid to a boil. Simmer for about 15 minutes. Strain out flavorings; bring the reserved liquid to a boil again. Add shrimp and cook until just cooked through (about 2 to 3 minutes). Remove shrimp from liquid and allow shrimp to cool.

Put red onions and olives in a bowl. Pour the hot cooking liquid over the red onions and olives. Marinate at room temperature for 1 hour. Add the shrimp to the onion mixture and refrigerate. When chilled, serve topped with fresh mint. ❧

# Orange-Fennel-Olive Salad

*Classic Mediterranean flavor combinations make this side salad memorable.*

MAKES 4 TO 6 SMALL SERVINGS

4 bulbs fresh fennel, core removed and julienned
1/4 cup extra virgin olive oil
2 oranges, cut in sections with white membrane removed
1/4 cup pitted black olives
2 tablespoons chopped fresh mint
juice of 1 lemon
1 teaspoon sea salt

Sauté the fennel on medium heat for about 1 minute in a few tablespoons of the olive oil. Transfer to a bowl and toss with all the other ingredients and the remaining olive oil. Serve at room temperature as a side dish with Sardinas al la Plancha (page 112), Gambas al Alcaparra (page 101) or Pez Espada (page 110). ❧

# Moroccan Eggplant

*Roasting the eggplant brings out its elusive flavor and gives it a deep, rich texture.*

MAKES 6 SERVINGS

1 large or 2 small eggplants
¼ cup olive oil for roasting
10 to 12 cloves of garlic
1 red bell or pimento pepper, roasted, peeled, and thinly sliced
2 teaspoons coarsely chopped fresh mint
1 teaspoon coriander seed, toasted and ground
¼ cup extra virgin olive oil for drizzling over the cooked eggplant
black olives

Preheat the oven to 375 degrees. Pierce eggplant liberally with a small, sharp paring knife and coat it with 4 to 6 tablespoons of the oil. Push garlic cloves deep into some of the slits. Place on a baking pan and bake for 25 minutes. Turn eggplant over and continue to cook for an additional 20 minutes, or until it is only slightly firm. Remove it from the oven and allow to cool at room temperature.

When eggplant has cooled enough to handle, remove the skin and coarsely chop the eggplant into bite-size chunks, then place them neatly in a shallow earthenware or glass pan for serving.

Garnish with roasted red pepper, sprinkle on the mint and coriander, and coat lightly with more olive oil. Serve accompanied with individual bowls of Mojo Verde (page 18) and black olives. Serve some Rosemary-Yogurt Flatbread (page 123) with this dish. ❧

# Tortilla Española

*Spanish Omelet*

*A traditional tapa, this Spanish omelet is made with potatoes and eggs and is served at room temperature with Romesco Sauce.*

MAKES 6 SERVINGS

1 medium-size onion, thinly sliced
1 cup olive oil
3 pounds (approximately 10) medium-size potatoes,
    peeled and sliced into 1/4-inch slices
6 eggs, beaten
1/4 tablespoon salt
Romesco Sauce (page 30)

Preheat oven to 350 degrees. Sauté the onion in 1/4 cup of olive oil until very soft and sweet. In a small roasting pan, toss potatoes with remaining oil, cover, and bake for 20 minutes. Uncover the pan and spread onion slices evenly over potatoes. Cover and bake for an additional 20 minutes. Remove the pan and pour off the oil, reserving it. Cool potatoes to room temperature. Season the eggs with salt and fold the potato-onion mixture into the eggs.

Heat a few tablespoons of the reserved oil in a nonstick sauté pan over high heat. When it's hot, carefully add the egg mixture. Allow the eggs to set on a high heat for a minute while gently shaking the pan so they don't stick. Reduce the heat to the lowest temperature and cook for 15 to 20 minutes, or until the mixture is firm.

Place plate on top (upside down as you look at it) of the sauté pan and flip the tortilla onto the plate. (Do this over your sink.) Reheat the skillet over high heat and carefully slide the tortilla back into the pan. Reduce the heat to low and cook the other side until it is done, about 8 minutes or until it feels firm to the touch.

Cool the tortilla to room temperature and slice it into wedges. When you are ready to serve, spoon some of the Romesco Sauce onto a plate and place wedge on top. ❧

# Tapas Calientes

# Espinaca con Pasas

*Sautéed Spinach with Raisins*

*A popular flavor combination in Mediterranean cooking, as well as a tasty vegetarian tapa or side dish. Try this as an empanada filling with Manchego cheese.*

MAKES 4 SERVINGS

$^1/_2$ cup golden raisins
$^1/_2$ cup fruity white wine
$^1/_4$ cup olive oil
1 red bell pepper, diced
4 cloves garlic, chopped
$^1/_2$ pound fresh spinach
$^1/_4$ cup pine nuts
salt and black pepper

Soak the raisins in the white wine for 4 hours to soften. Heat olive oil in a sauté pan on medium heat. Sauté pepper for 2 minutes and then add garlic. Add the raisin and wine mixture. Add the spinach and stir gently until cooked, about 3 minutes. Remove from heat and toss with pine nuts, salt, and pepper. ❧

# Gambas al Ajillo

*Sautéed Garlic Shrimp with Lime and Madeira*

*This is the most popular tapa at El Farol!*

½ white onion, chopped
¼ cup olive oil
1 pound large shrimp, peeled and deveined
6 cloves garlic, minced
4 green onions, chopped
3 tablespoons Madeira wine
juice of one lime
1 teaspoon paprika
½ teaspoon cayenne pepper
½ cup Chicken Stock (page 37), flavored with bay leaf
salt to taste
chopped fresh parsley (optional)

Sauté white onion in olive oil on high heat until soft; add shrimp and garlic. Sauté for 1 minute. Remove shrimp from pan and set aside. Add all other ingredients except parsley and cook down for 2 minutes. Remove the pan from heat, add shrimp and toss them with the sauce. Serve on a platter, topped with chopped fresh parsley. ❧

# Bonito

*Almond-Crusted Seared Tuna with Toasted Cumin Tomato Sauce*

*I love rare and raw tuna in almost any preparation. This one has some Spanish flair with tomatoes, almonds, and cumin. Toasting the cumin seeds accentuates the flavor and aroma of the sauce. You may never buy ground spices again!*

1 pound fresh tuna
1/4 cup olive oil
1 handful of sliced almonds
1/2 teaspoon paprika
1 teaspoon minced garlic
salt and pepper
Toasted Cumin Tomato Sauce (page 27)

Cut tuna into 4-ounce pieces and drizzle with a few tablespoons of olive oil. Mix almonds, paprika, garlic, salt, and pepper in a bowl. Toss tuna pieces with almond mixture until the fish is well coated. Heat the remaining olive oil in a sauté pan on medium-high heat. Sear the tuna for about 2 minutes per side. Remove from pan and serve immediately with Toasted Cumin Tomato Sauce. ✍

Portobellos en Jerez

# Portobellos en Jerez
*Mushrooms Simmered in Sherry*

*One of El Farol's most popular tapas from the recipe archives. Oyster mushrooms work well here, as do regular button mushrooms.*

MAKES 4 TAPA SERVINGS

1/4 cup good olive oil
1/2 yellow onion, peeled and diced
2 green onions, chopped
6 cloves garlic, minced
4 large portobello mushroom caps, cut in 1-inch dice
1 tablespoon sherry vinegar
1 cup dry Spanish sherry
1 tablespoon fresh thyme
salt and black pepper to taste

Heat oil on high in a sauté pan. Add onions, garlic, and mushrooms. Sauté, stirring occasionally, for 2 minutes. Add all other ingredients and bring to a boil. Turn down to simmer for 5 minutes. Serve hot as a tapa. ❧

# Pasta Piñon Verde

*Bow Tie Pasta with Pine Nuts, Cream, and Poblano Chiles*

*Sometimes a creamy, cheesy pasta dish just feels right. Local piñons from the short, twisted piñon trees are buttery smooth pine nuts that make this dish extra rich and nutty. The Mexican poblano chile provides this tapa with a citrusy heat to balance things out.*

MAKES 8 SMALL PLATES OF PASTA AS A TAPA

2 quarts of water

pinch of salt

1 pound farfalle (bow tie) pasta

1/2 yellow onion, diced

1 tablespoon minced fresh garlic

1/8 cup butter

3 tablespoons white wine

1 pint heavy cream

2 poblano chiles, roasted, peeled, and chopped

1 handful of shelled piñons or pine nuts

1/2 cup grated Manchego or Parmesan cheese

salt and cracked black pepper to taste

2 tomatoes, diced

Boil 2 quarts of water with a pinch of salt. Cook pasta for about 8 to 10 minutes or until al dente. While pasta is cooking, sauté onion and garlic in butter until soft, and then deglaze the pan with white wine. Add cream, poblano chiles, and piñons to the sauté pan and bring to a boil. Cook on high heat for about 2 minutes. Turn off the heat and stir in the cheese. Drain the pasta and, while it is still hot, toss it with the cream sauce. Add salt and pepper and serve topped with diced fresh tomatoes. ❧

# Higos Rellenos
## Cabrales-Stuffed Fresh Figs

*This is on the menu at El Farol in early summer when the fresh black mission figs are at their best. A classic European fruit and cheese combination, this tapa is easy to make and offers a mouthful of well-blended flavors. The figs are stuffed with pecans and Cabrales cheese, then wrapped in jamon serrano and grilled.*

MAKES 24 SERVINGS

12 fresh figs
1/2 cup crumbled Cabrales (or other blue cheese)
24 pecan halves
12 very thin slices of jamon serrano or prosciutto, cut in half lengthwise

Cut figs in half from top to bottom. Into each half, press a teaspoon of Cabrales and a pecan half. Wrap each fig half with a strip of jamon. Grill on medium heat for only 1 minute. Serve immediately with Vinagre de Jerez (page 17) or Pedro Ximenez Caramel Sauce (page 172).

# Argentine Beef Empanadas
## Beef Turnovers

*Pastry turnovers stuffed with an endless variety of meats, fish, and fruits are popular in almost all Spanish-speaking areas of the world, especially in Spain, Argentina, Mexico, and New Mexico.*

MAKES 20 EMPANADAS

**Empanada Dough**

1 1/2 cups flour

1 cup masa harina (finely ground cornmeal)

1/2 teaspoon paprika

1 teaspoon baking powder

1 teaspoon salt

1/2 cup unsalted butter, melted

1/2 to 3/4 cup of water

1 large egg beaten with 1 tablespoon water, for egg wash

**To Make Dough:**

In a large bowl, sift together the dry ingredients. Stir in the melted butter. Gradually work in the water with your hands; the dough should be easy to handle and not sticky. Form the dough into a ball, wrap it in plastic, and chill for 30 minutes.

Lightly flour a rolling pin and counter. Divide the dough in half and roll it out to 1/8-inch thickness. Using a 4-inch cookie or biscuit cutter, cut out 20 circles of dough; repeat with the other half.

Making Empanadas

**Filling**

6 portobello mushrooms

¼ cup olive oil

4 cloves garlic, sliced thin

1 teaspoon chopped fresh thyme leaves

1 tablespoon sherry vinegar

¼ cup amontillado sherry

salt and black pepper to taste

½ cup crumbled Cabrales (or other blue cheese)

**To Make Filling:**

Cut the mushrooms into ¼-inch dice and sauté in olive oil for about 3 minutes. Add the garlic, thyme, sherry vinegar, and sherry. Cook for about 3 more minutes; season with salt and pepper. Set aside and cool to room temperature. Fold in the blue cheese after mixture has reached room temperature.

**To Assemble:**

Preheat oven to 400 degrees. Lay out all pastry circles on a lightly floured work surface. Working one at a time, brush egg wash around the outer edge of the circle. This will help seal the edges. Place a tablespoon of the mushroom mixture in the center of each pastry circle. Fold the pastry into a half-moon shape and pinch the edges together with your fingers. Crimp the edges with a fork. Brush each empanada with egg wash. Place on a lightly oiled baking sheet and bake for 8 to 10 minutes or until nicely browned. ৶

# Chorizo-Potato Empanadas

*Sausage-Potato Turnovers*

*The filling for these empanadas can also be used as an enchilada filling, pizza topping, or cooked with scrambled eggs for breakfast.*

MAKES **16** EMPANADAS

**Empanada Dough**

1 1/2 cups flour

1 cup masa harina (finely ground cornmeal)

1/2 teaspoon paprika

1 teaspoon baking powder

1 teaspoon salt

1/2 cup unsalted butter, melted

1/2 to 3/4 cup of water

1 large egg beaten with 1 tablespoon water, for egg wash

**To Make Dough:**

In a large bowl, sift together the dry ingredients. Stir in the melted butter. Gradually work in the water with your hands; the dough should be easy to handle and not sticky. Form the dough into a ball, wrap it in plastic, and chill for 30 minutes.

Lightly flour a rolling pin and counter. Divide the dough in half and roll it out to 1/8-inch thickness. Using a 4-inch cookie or biscuit cutter, cut out 16 circles of dough; repeat with the other half.

**Filling**

1½ cups chopped chorizo

¼ cup Sofrito (page 3)

2 cups diced potatoes

2 tablespoons olive oil

½ cup chopped cilantro for garnish

**To Make Filling:**

Boil the potatoes in salted water until soft, about 15 minutes. Drain and set aside. On medium heat, sauté the chopped chorizo. Stir and cook until browned and some fat is rendered. Remove chorizo with a slotted spoon and set aside. Add the Sofrito to the pan with the chorizo fat and sauté for 2 minutes. Add the cooked potatoes. Add the chorizo and stir well. Remove from heat and cool to room temperature.

**To Assemble:**

Preheat oven to 400 degrees. Lay out all pastry circles on a lightly floured work surface. Working one at a time, brush egg wash around the outer edge of the circle. This will help seal the edges. Place a tablespoon of the chorizo-potato mixture in the center of each pastry circle. Fold the pastry into a half-moon shape and pinch the edges together with your fingers. Crimp the edges with a fork. Brush each empanada with egg wash. Place on a lightly oiled baking sheet and bake for 8 to 10 minutes or until nicely browned.

# Gambas al Alcaparra
## Grilled Honey-Caper Shrimp

*Grilling shrimp in this simple sweet-and-sour emulsion creates an exotic Mediterranean flavor combination that will have your friends asking for the recipe.*

MAKES 4 SERVINGS

1 pound large shrimp, peeled and deveined
3 tablespoons capers
2 tablespoons pickling liquid from the jar of capers
1/2 cup honey
2 tablespoons dry sherry
zest of 1 lemon
juice of 1/2 lemon
2 teaspoons sea salt
1 1/2 cups extra virgin olive oil
capers for garnish
lemon wedges for garnish

Put shrimp in a glass baking dish or bowl. In a food processor, puree all remaining ingredients except olive oil and garnishes to make the marinade. While the motor is running, add olive oil in a slow, steady stream. Toss shrimp with this marinade and refrigerate for 1 hour. Grill over medium-hot coals for about 2 minutes per side. Serve 3 to 4 hot shrimp per person, dressing each plate with capers and lemon wedges. ✎

# Puerco Asado

*Grilled Marinated Whole Pork Tenderloin*

*As with many of the marinades we use at El Farol, we suggest allowing 24 hours for the flavors to penetrate the meat. This is a very basic preparation for pork that is cooked over coals or seared in a hot pan, then finished in the oven. The cooked pork can be sliced in medallions and served immediately, or cooled and sliced for sandwiches. We serve this with Port-Fig Syrup and shavings of Idiazabel cheese.*

MAKES **8** TAPA SERVINGS

1 whole pork tenderloin, trimmed of silvery skin
¼ cup olive oil
½ tablespoon coriander seed, cracked and toasted
4 cloves garlic, peeled and smashed
1 cup apple cider
2 tablespoons Dijon mustard
2 tablespoons sherry vinegar
2 tablespoons brown sugar
2 teaspoons kosher salt
2 tablespoons finely chopped parsley
2 tablespoons finely chopped fresh mint
pinch of cracked black pepper

Combine all ingredients except tenderloins to make marinade. Pour mixture over pork until the meat is covered. Refrigerate for 24 hours. Prepare a charcoal or gas grill or a cast-iron skillet. It should be a high temperature in order to caramelize the sugars in the marinade and seal in the moisture. Preheat oven to 400 degrees. Remove pork from marinade, sprinkle with a little more salt and pepper, and grill or sear the meat on all sides for about 5 minutes. Transfer pork to a baking sheet and finish cooking in the oven for 10 to 12 minutes. This will take the pork to a medium temperature; you can cook longer if you wish. Slice in ¼-inch slices and serve with Port-Fig Syrup (page 26). Garnish with shavings of Idiazabel cheese or other sharp cheese. ❧

# Albondigas

*Lamb Meatballs with Piñon and Mint*

*We make these with freshly ground New Mexican lamb meat, but you could easily substitute ground beef, turkey, veal, or pork, or try a combination of meats. This tapa has a Mediterranean flair, especially when we serve it with Mediterranean Couscous Salad (page 67).*

MAKES 24 SMALL MEATBALLS

2 pounds ground lamb

2 whole eggs

1 cup bread crumbs

$1/2$ cup toasted piñon nuts, crushed

$1/2$ cup chopped fresh mint

$1/2$ cup chopped Italian parsley

1 tablespoon coriander, toasted and ground

$1/2$ tablespoon cumin seed, toasted and ground

2 tablespoons tomato paste

6 cloves garlic, minced

1 tablespoon kosher salt

$1/2$ tablespoon cracked black pepper

In a large bowl, mix all ingredients well by hand or with a wooden spoon. Chill for 1 hour. Preheat oven to 375 degrees. Roll meat mixture into golf-ball-size meatballs and arrange on a baking sheet. Cover with foil and bake for 30 minutes. Remove from oven and serve 2 per person with Romesco Sauce (page 30).

# Pulpo Asado
Grilled Octopus

I was afraid this was going to be one of those menu items that the staff loves but customers avoid. I tried it anyway, and, as it so often happens, I was proven wrong. It has become such a staple that we cannot take it off the menu. The key to tenderizing octopus is to cook it in simmering broth for 4 to 5 hours. (You must put a wine cork in the water while cooking the octopus, and quite honestly, it works. I cannot tell you why or how—just do as I say!) Most cooks make the mistake of undercooking because after 1 to 2 hours, the octopus becomes very tough and rubbery and they think it's overcooked. It's not. Don't stop. Keep going.

MAKES 4 TO 6 SERVINGS AS A TAPA

2 small octopuses (cleaned), usually found frozen, which will be fine
2 gallons water
1 tablespoon crushed red chile flakes
4 cloves garlic
1 tablespoon sea salt
1 teaspoon cracked black pepper
1 wine cork

Put all ingredients in large pot and bring to a boil. Boil for 15 minutes and then turn down to a high simmer for 4 1/2 hours. Remove octopuses from liquid and cool to room temperature. Cut each octopus into 4 pieces. Marinate.

**For Marinade:**

1/2 yellow onion, minced
6 cloves garlic, minced
2 roma tomatoes, diced
2 tablespoons chopped Italian parsley
1 teaspoon hot smoked paprika
1 teaspoon capers

juice of 1 lemon
2 tablespoons brown sugar
1 tablespoon tomato paste
salt and pepper
1/2 cup extra virgin olive oil

Mix ingredients in a bowl and toss well with cooked octopuses. Marinate for 3 to 4 hours for quick use or overnight for more depth of flavor. Heat a charcoal grill to medium-high temperature. Grill on all sides for a total grilling time of 4 to 5 minutes. The outer edges of the tentacles should be slightly charred and blackened. Serve hot off the grill, drizzled with extra virgin olive oil and Moroccan Olive Pesto (page 9); garnish with lemon wedges. ◞

# Queso Frito

*Goat Cheese and Ham Fritters*

*A good fresh, local goat cheese with a firm texture will work with this recipe. We are blessed in New Mexico with cheeses from Sweetwoods Dairy in Peña Blanca.*

MAKES 12 FRITTERS

1 yellow onion, diced

3 scallions, chopped

4 cloves garlic, minced

2 tablespoons chopped fresh rosemary

1/2 cup chopped ham

4 tablespoons olive oil

2 cups fresh goat cheese

1 tablespoon Dijon mustard

cracked black pepper to taste

1 pint vegetable or peanut oil for frying

1/4 cup cornstarch

Sauté onion, scallions, garlic, rosemary, and ham in olive oil until onions are soft. Let cool. Blend goat cheese with the onion mixture, mustard, and black pepper. Chill well for about an hour. Heat vegetable oil in a deep pot to 350 degrees. Form mixture by hand into 12 small round cakes. Dredge cakes in cornstarch until they are completely coated. Fry 2 at a time for about 30 seconds, or until outer coating gets a little crispy, but be careful that the cheese does not start to melt. Serve warm with fresh green salad and bread. ❧

# Croquetas de Salmone

*Smoked Salmon Potato Cakes*

*Cook the potatoes until very soft and starchy—this will help hold the cakes together.*

MAKES 20 CAKES

10 to 12 diced red potatoes, skin on, boiled until soft
2 cups diced smoked salmon
1/2 cup chopped cornichons (specialty pickles)
1/4 cup chopped parsley
2 tablespoons Dijon mustard
3/4 cup mayonnaise
1 red bell pepper, diced
4 green onions, chopped
1 cup bread crumbs, plus extra for dredging
1 teaspoon cayenne pepper
salt and pepper
1 1/2 quarts vegetable oil for deep frying

Fold all ingredients except extra bread crumbs together in a mixing bowl. Chill for 2 hours. Form mixture into 20 (2-inch) cakes and dredge in more bread crumbs. Heat vegetable oil in a deep skillet to about 375 degrees and deep-fry 2 cakes at a time for about 1 minute each. Serve with Green Olive Vinaigrette (page 14).

# Croquetas de Bacaloa

*Salt Cod Potato Cakes*

Almost as important as fresh fish
in Spanish and Portuguese cooking
is the ever-present salt-cured cod,
bacaloa. There are hundreds of
ways to serve it; this is one of the
simplest and my personal favorite.
Fried croquettes of salt cod cooked
with milk and onions are delicious
hot from the frying pan, but they
also can be eaten cold or packed
for a picnic. I learned this dish
from Chef Sam Clark, whose
restaurant, Moro, in London,
serves authentic tapas and
Mediterranean food. We were in
Sanlucar de Barrameda when Sam
made these croquettes for a cooking demo. We carried the little
fried goodies to the Hidalgo sherry
bodega and sampled sherries in
the tasting room as we passed the
plate of croquettes. It was one of
my all-time great food and wine
experiences.

MAKES 6 TAPA SERVINGS

1 pound of salt cod

2 cups milk

2 yellow onions, finely diced

2 bay leaves

6 new potatoes, diced

1 cup chopped Italian flat-leaf parsley

small pinch of ground clove

1 teaspoon flour

1/2 cup chopped jamon serrano
   (optional)

salt and cracked black pepper to taste

4 cups vegetable oil for frying

Soak the salt cod for at least 24 hours in water in the refrigerator, changing the
water 2 to 3 times in that 24-hour period. Put the salt cod in a saucepan with the
milk, 1 of the diced onions, and the bay leaves. Bring to a boil and then turn
down to a simmer for 3 to 4 minutes. Remove the salt cod with a slotted spoon
and set aside. Keep simmering the milk mixture and add the potatoes; cook until
soft, about 15 minutes.

Flake the salt cod and remove any bones and hard pieces of skin. Drain the potatoes, transfer to a bowl, and mash with a fork. Add the shredded salt cod, the other
diced onion, parsley, clove, flour, and chopped jamon if using. Blend well. Taste for
seasoning; it may need a little salt and it will take some cracked black pepper.

Heat the oil to about 350 degrees. Shape the croquettes between two spoons:
make small oval shapes by scooping some mixture with one spoon and shaping it
with the other until you get a firm semi-smooth shape. Transfer to a floured surface. (At this point you could refrigerate the croquettes for up to 24 hours. They
do better in the frying oil when they are well chilled.) Deep-fry 4 to 5 at a time
until golden brown, about 1 minute, and transfer to a plate lined with paper towels.
Serve with a nice dry sherry and some Lemon-Caper Aioli (page 5). ෴

# Pinchos de Venado

*Grilled Venison Skewers*

*Serve these grilled skewers with apple–red wine compote or Aioli de Higos (page 6).*

(page 6)

MAKES 6 TAPA SERVINGS

2 pounds fresh venison or beef

$1/4$ cup honey

$1/4$ cup sherry vinegar

2 tablespoons minced garlic

1 tablespoon chopped fresh rosemary

2 tablespoons molasses

$1/4$ cup tomato juice

2 tablespoons chopped parsley

$1/4$ cup apple cider or juice

6 (6-inch) bamboo or metal skewers

Cut the meat into 24 (1-inch) cubes. Toss the meat with all other ingredients to marinate. Set in the refrigerator, covered, for 24 hours. Light a charcoal grill. Put 4 pieces of meat on skewers and grill on all sides over medium heat, about 10 minutes total. ❧

# Pez Espada
## Moroccan-Spiced Swordfish Skewers

*A lively North African spice combo makes this tapa aromatic.*

MAKES 10 SKEWERS

2¹/₂ pounds fresh swordfish or blue marlin
10 (6-inch) bamboo or metal skewers
¹/₄ cup El Farol Pincho Spice Mix (page 36)
2 tablespoons fresh lime juice
6 cloves garlic
¹/₄ cup packed fresh cilantro, chopped
¹/₂ cup olive oil
1 tablespoon kosher salt
rice or couscous

Cut the fish into 40 large cubes and thread 4 pieces on each bamboo or metal skewer.

In a bowl mix all ingredients well and pour over skewered fish in a nonreactive container. Marinate in the refrigerator for 4 to 5 hours. Light a charcoal grill and when it is hot, grill the fish over medium heat on all sides until firm, about 8 minutes total. Serve over a bed of rice or Mediterranean Couscous Salad (page 67).

# Almejas con Manzanilla

*Clams Steamed in Sherry with Fennel Seed*

*A classic tapa of steamed clams that is elevated by the briny flavor of Manzanilla, a dry fino from Sanlucar de Barrameda, and toasted fennel seeds.*

MAKES 6 TAPA SERVINGS

1 tablespoon fennel seeds
4 pounds fresh clams
1 cup Manzanilla
1 cup bottled clam juice
1/2 cup chopped Italian parsley
1/4 cup chopped green onions
1 tablespoon minced garlic
2 tablespoons butter
1 tablespoon olive oil
salt to taste (optional)

Toast fennel seeds in a hot, dry skillet until browned and smoking. Remove from heat. Put the clams in a deep skillet with the remaining ingredients. Cover and cook at high heat until the clams pop open. Check the broth for seasoning. Sometimes the clams will not need salt, but you can add it if you like. Discard any clams that don't open. Serve with cold beer or a glass of Manzanilla. ❧

# Sardinas al la Plancha

*Grilled Fresh Portuguese Sardines*

*Any flavorful small fish will work here, such as herring, smelt, small ocean perch, or large anchovies. The plancha is a flat iron cooking surface or flat grill. A good cast-iron pan is the best way to create your own plancha. Try these little sea treasures with Orange-Fennel-Olive Salad (page 76) and Lemon-Caper Aioli (page 5) and you will be transported to the Portuguese coast.*

MAKES 12 TAPA SERVINGS

12 whole sardines, cleaned and deboned (leave skin on)
1/2 cup good Spanish olive oil
8 cloves garlic, minced
1/4 cup chopped Italian parsley
juice of 1 lemon
zest of 1 lemon
pinch of sea salt

Put all ingredients except fish in a bowl and mix together. Toss fish with the mixture and chill for 20 minutes. In a cast-iron pan over medium heat, cook the fillets skin-side-up for 1 minute and flip to cook the other side for another minute. Serve immediately with above suggestions and a nice chilled *vino verde*.

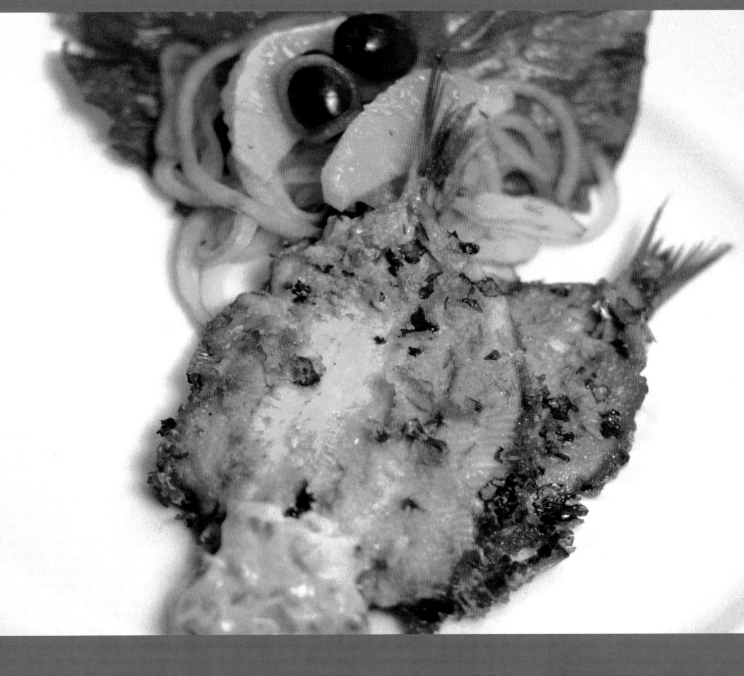

# El Farol Fried Calamari

*We make our fried calamari light and crispy with rice flour and Japanese bread crumbs.*

MAKES 6 TAPA SERVINGS

1½ pounds cleaned calamari, fresh or frozen
3 cups whole milk
¼ cup chopped fresh parsley
2 quarts vegetable oil for frying
2 cups rice flour
6 eggs, beaten
1 tablespoon kosher salt
1 teaspoon cracked black pepper
2 cups Panko Japanese bread crumbs

Cut the calamari bodies into ¼-inch rings and remove the tentacles. Put rings and tentacles in the milk and stir in the parsley. Allow to marinate for 2 to 3 hours in the refrigerator.

Heat the oil to about 350 degrees or until a cube of bread turns golden brown in about 12 seconds when placed in hot oil. Remove calamari from milk and discard the milk. Toss calamari with the rice flour until well-coated; transfer to a bowl and toss with the eggs until well-coated. Sprinkle with a little bit of the salt and all of the black pepper. Transfer to another bowl and toss with the bread crumbs until well-coated and dry enough to separate each piece. Add more bread crumbs if needed.

Fry in batches in hot oil 20 to 30 seconds or until light brown and crispy. Remove with a slotted spoon. Do not overcook. Transfer to paper towels and sprinkle with kosher salt. Serve with Lemon-Caper Aioli (page 5) and Romesco Sauce (page 30) for dipping; garnish with wedges of lime.

# Pollo Harissa
*Chicken with Harissa*

*Roasted chicken with cinnamon and cloves has an exotic scent and makes a perfect match for our fiery Harissa Sauce.*

MAKES 8 TAPAS

8 chicken thighs or breasts with skin (or skin-on breasts)
2 tablespoons ground canela or cinnamon
1 tablespoon ground cloves
1 tablespoon ground coriander
1 tablespoon grated orange peel
juice of 2 oranges
2 tablespoons minced garlic
1/4 cup honey
1/4 cup olive oil
1/4 cup oloroso sherry
1 tablespoon salt
1 teaspoon cracked black pepper

Toss the raw chicken with all other ingredients and allow to marinate in the refrigerator for 24 hours. Preheat oven to 450 degrees. Put chicken in a single layer in a glass baking dish and roast uncovered for 20 minutes. Turn oven down to 350; cover chicken with foil and roast for another 15 minutes or until chicken is cooked through. Serve one thigh or breast per plate as a tapa, with Harissa Sauce (page 24) and Rosemary-Yogurt Flatbread (page 123). ◠

Aguacate

# Aguacate
*Crispy Fried Avocado*

*One of our popular new-world tapas. It sounds unusual to have a cooked avocado; however, it fries quickly, which gets the coating nice and crispy and the avocado just barely warm in the middle.*

MAKES 4 TAPA SERVINGS

2 quarts vegetable oil for deep frying
2 avocados
3/4 cup Panko Japanese bread crumbs
1/4 cup yellow cornmeal
salt and pepper
1 cup flour
4 eggs, beaten

Heat cooking oil in a deep pan to about 350 degrees. Cut avocados in half, remove pits, and peel. Mix bread crumbs, cornmeal, salt, and pepper in a bowl. Dredge peeled avocado halves in flour, then in eggs, then in bread crumb mixture. Fry until crispy and golden brown, about 1 minute. Serve on a bed of greens with Chipotle-Mustard Vinaigrette (page 16), sour cream, and Pickled Red Onions (page 19). ❧

# Achiote Citrus-Steamed Chicken in Banana Leaf
## Marinated Chicken Cooked in Banana Leaves

This is another new-world tapa with lively flavors of Mexico. Achiote paste is made from ground annatto seed; it is a Latin American specialty item.

MAKES 8 SERVINGS

juice of 4 oranges
juice of 2 limes
2 tablespoons achiote paste
4 cloves garlic, minced
1 tablespoon salt
4 (4-ounce) chicken breasts, boneless, skinless, and cut in half
8 pieces of banana leaf, cut in 4-inch squares for wrapping and 8 strips for tying

Combine fruit juices with achiote paste, garlic, and salt; mix well. Toss with chicken and marinate for 1 hour. Place a chicken piece in the center of each piece of banana leaf and drizzle with remaining marinade. Enclose by folding the sides in and then the tops and bottoms of the leaves, and secure with the strip piece, wrapping around once and tying.

These bundles can now be placed on a grill at medium heat for 4 minutes per side; the chicken will steam in its juices. ☙

# Hojas de Uva

*Crispy Fried Grape Leaves*

*I created this as a garnish for a special wine dinner to tie into the "grape" theme. Hojas de Uva can give the plate dramatic and unusual presentation because the leaves become crispy, shiny, and translucent. Frying also deepens and softens the flavor of the tangy leaves, so they are a tasty, edible garnish. I have them on hand and find myself munching on them and crumbling them into other dishes. They are delicious.*

MAKES 8 CRISPY LEAVES AS AN EDIBLE GARNISH

3 cups vegetable oil for deep frying
8 grape leaves (from the jar, not fresh—fresh leaves will not work)

Heat oil to about 350 degrees. Fry the leaves one at a time by laying the leaf on the surface of the hot oil. Cook for 15 seconds and then turn the leaf over with tongs and fry for about 10 seconds. The leaves may not seem rigid and crispy, but they will be after they cool. Transfer to a plate lined with paper towels and cool. Continue with each leaf. For more of a grape leaf cup, hold a small ladle down on the leaf as it is frying to give it shape.

# Pimientos de Padron

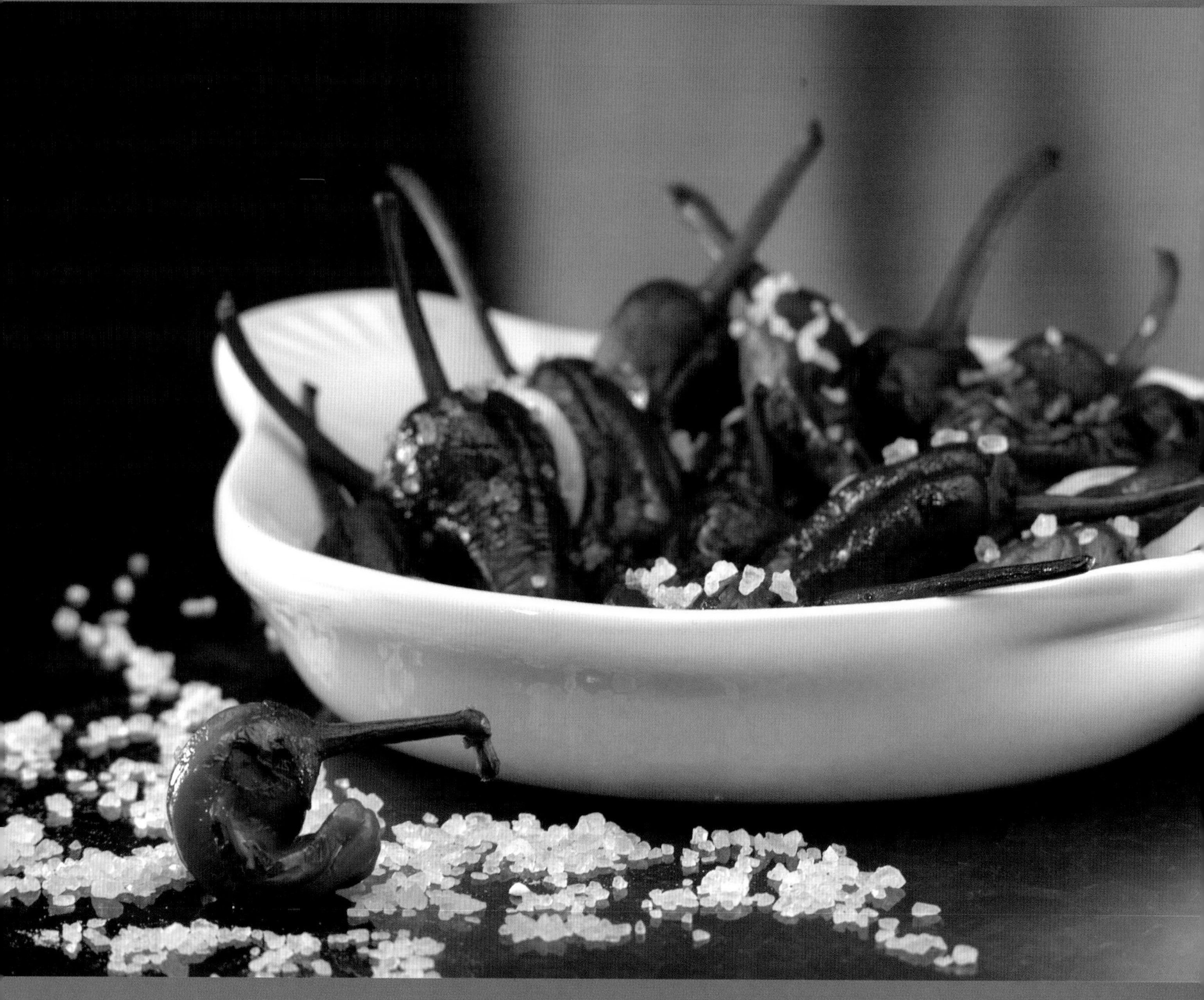

# Pimientos de Padron

*Chiles with Sea Salt*

*This recipe uses a very flavorful and unusual thumb-size fresh green chile from Spain that is being grown in small amounts in the U.S. (see Pantry Items, page 191). They are very difficult to find. Of course, in Santa Fe they sell quickly because our customers are always up for a new chile sensation. These chiles have a sweet, earthy, mild flavor, but beware: every so often there is a scorching hot one in the bunch. You can substitute poblano chiles that have a similar flavor but are much larger and require more cooking time.*

MAKES 6 TAPA SERVINGS

1/2 cup olive oil
1 1/2 pounds pimientos de padron, or 6 small poblano chiles
4 garlic cloves, peeled and sliced thin
1 tablespoon sea salt

Heat a cast-iron skillet and add a few tablespoons of olive oil. Add the chiles and cook, stirring until the skins are blackened and blistered and the chiles collapse. Add the garlic and sea salt and fry until brown. Transfer to a platter and drizzle with remaining olive oil. Pass the cold beer or fino sherry and bread. ✑

# Pepita Flatbread

*Pepitas are the green seeds of a Latin American squash (or little green pumpkins or calabasa.) The seeds have a rich, nutty flavor and are used often in cooking. We like the earthy flavor of this flatbread that is served with queso de cabra— hot, bubbling, baked goat cheese.*

MAKES ABOUT 20 PIECES

2¼ cups flour
1 cup cornmeal
2 teaspoons salt
¼ teaspoon cayenne pepper
⅓ cup butter
1 cup warm water
1 teaspoon yeast
2 teaspoons sugar
2 eggs, beaten
1 cup pepitas, toasted and crushed

Mix flour, cornmeal, salt, and cayenne pepper. Melt butter and set aside. Mix water, yeast, and sugar separately. Mix melted butter and sugar-and-yeast mixture into the dry ingredients and knead into a dough. Allow the dough to rise for 1 hour at room temperature. On a floured surface, roll the dough into a 12-inch flat circle, about ¼-inch thick. Brush with beaten eggs and top with crushed pepitas. Brush more egg over the pepitas. Cut the circle into 20 long wedges. Transfer wedges to a lightly oiled baking sheet. Bake at 350 degrees for 10 to 12 minutes.

# Rosemary-Yogurt Flatbread

*This is a delicious chewy bread that goes well with many foods. Serve with Pollo Harissa (page 115), paellas (pages 133–37), or Grilled Quail with Espresso-Chipotle Sauce (page 153).*

MAKES 12 (6-INCH) ROUND FLATBREADS

4 cups all-purpose flour
1 tablespoon finely chopped fresh rosemary
1 teaspoon baking powder
1 teaspoon sea salt
2 cups plain yogurt
1 tablespoon vegetable oil
2 tablespoons extra virgin olive oil

Mix dry ingredients in a large bowl. Stir in yogurt. Knead until a smooth dough forms. In a lightly oiled bowl, let dough rest at room temperature for about an hour, covered with a damp cloth.

Cut dough into 12 pieces and roll each piece into a ball. Then roll each piece flat, about 1/4-inch thick and 6 inches in diameter. Heat a cast-iron skillet lightly oiled with vegetable oil. Cook one piece of bread at a time for about 2 minutes on the first side, then flip and cook for 1 minute on the other side. Serve hot, drizzled with hearty Moroccan extra virgin olive oil. Also works well served with Moroccan Eggplant (page 77). ∾

Mejillones con Jamon

# Mejillones con Jamon
*Steamed Black Mussels with Carrots and Jamon Serrano in a Dijon-Sherry Cream Sauce*

*This is another variation of the great Spanish tradition of mixing meats with seafood—mar y montano.*

MAKES 6 TAPA SERVINGS

1/2 cup julienned carrots

2 pounds fresh black mussels, debearded

1/4 cup chopped jamon serrano

1 tablespoon chopped garlic

1 tablespoon Dijon mustard

1 cup dry fino

1/2 cup heavy cream

Cut carrots into matchstick-sized pieces. Place all ingredients in a shallow pan on high heat and cover. Cook just until mussels open (discard any mussels that do not open). Stir well and serve with lots of crusty bread.

**Note:** The dish probably will not need salt, as the mussels and jamon tend to be salty enough.

# Alcachofas

*Grilled Artichokes in Saffron Butter*

*This is quickly becoming one of our most popular tapas. Small fresh artichokes work best because they are more tender. First, trim all outer leaves and then cut in half. With the small size, you won't have to worry about removing the choke because it will be tender. Remember to peel the long stem, but do not remove it. It is meaty and very flavorful. While peeling and trimming, rub the trimmed areas with half of a lemon to keep the leaves from turning brown or black.*

MAKES 4 SERVINGS

juice of 1 lemon
8 small artichokes, trimmed, peeled, and cut in half lengthwise
1/4 cup olive oil
2 tablespoons sherry vinegar
salt
1 cup butter
juice of 1 orange
pinch of Spanish saffron
6 cloves garlic

Bring 2 quarts of salted water to a boil and add juice of 1 lemon. Blanch the artichokes for 4 minutes. Transfer to a bowl of ice water to cool. Dry on paper towels. Toss with olive oil, vinegar, and a pinch of salt. Let marinate at room temperature for 4 hours.

In a saucepan, add butter, orange juice, saffron, and garlic. Bring the butter to a boil slowly—don't let it get too brown. Remove from heat without stirring and set aside. The butter solids will stay at the bottom. Pour the top layer of clarified butter into a bowl and discard the solids.

Light a charcoal or wood fire grill. Grill the artichokes at high heat for about 3 minutes per side until well marked. Transfer to a platter, pour on the clarified saffron butter, and serve. ໑

# Alcachofas

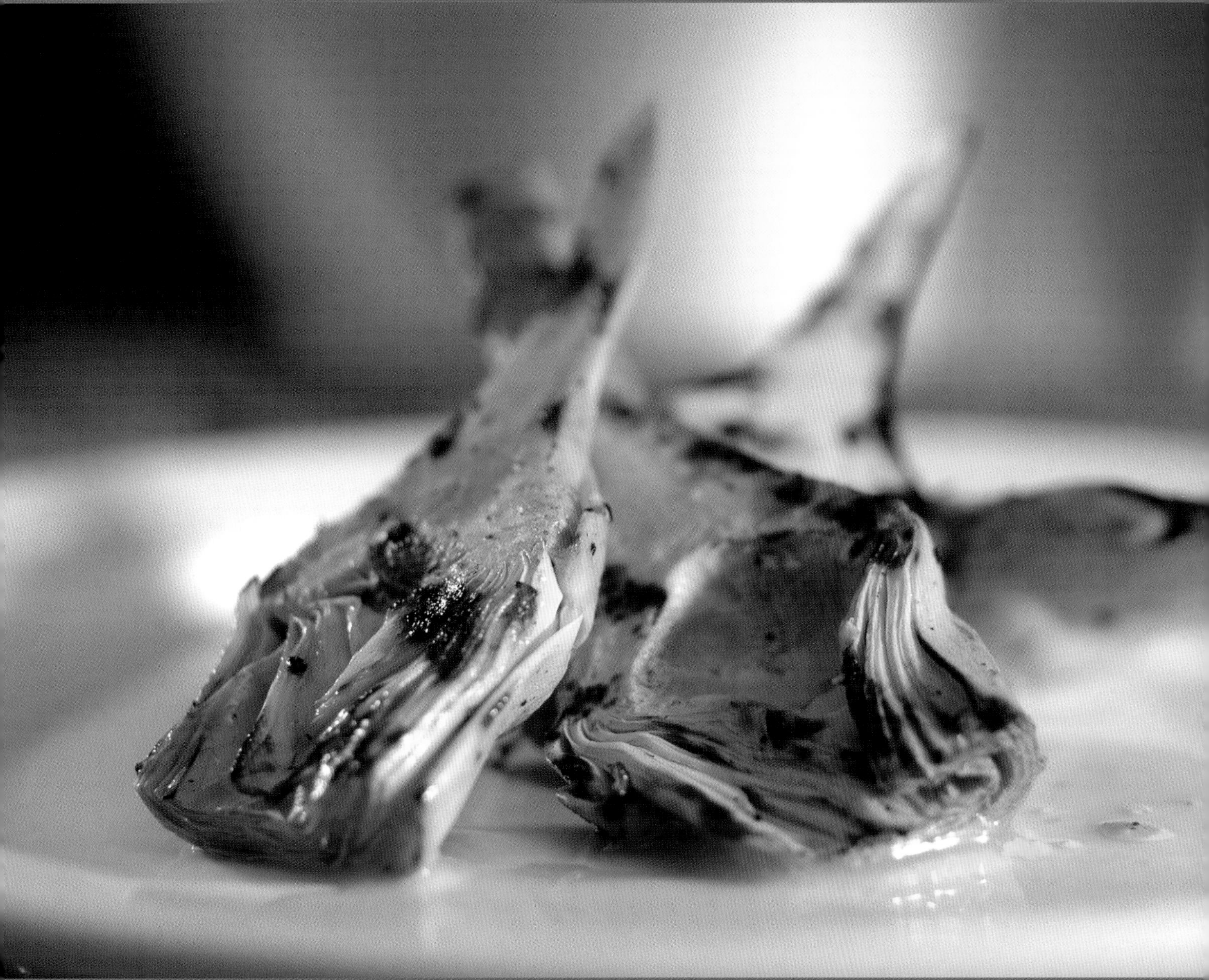

# Patatas Bravas

*Oven-Roasted Garlic Potatoes*

*This simple hot tapa can be served with a variety of dipping sauces such as Lemon-Caper Aioli (page 5), Harissa Sauce (page 24), or Romesco Sauce (page 30). It's also a tasty side dish for an entrée.*

MAKES 4 TAPA OR SIDE SERVINGS

2 pounds Yukon gold potatoes
3/4 cup olive oil
8 cloves of garlic, minced
2 tablespoons chopped parsley
1 tablespoon red chile pepper flakes
salt and black pepper to taste

Preheat oven to 375 degrees. Scrub potatoes. Toss potatoes and all other ingredients in a bowl to coat the potatoes well. Evenly place potatoes on a sheet pan and cover with aluminum foil; roast for 30 minutes. Uncover and let bake for another 15 minutes. Add more salt and pepper to taste. Serve hot with suggested sauces.

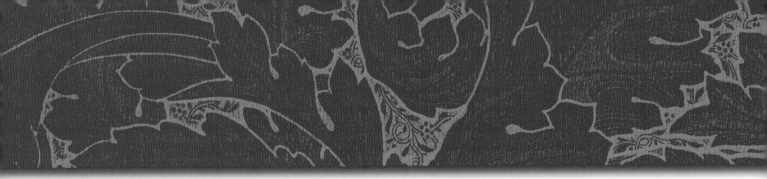

# Main Courses

# Paella de Puerco y Espinaca

*Pork and Spinach Rice Dish*

*The Phoenicians were the first group to introduce rice cultivation in the warm, wet Levante region of Spain. Calasparra rice or Bomba rice have a medium-short grain. It is not quite as short and starchy as Italian arborio rice but definitely more so than long-grain rice. These have become the favored rices for paella.*

*Not all paellas contain seafood. This one is hearty and flavorful. Try cooking two or three different types for a paella party.*

MAKES 4 SERVINGS

1 pound pork tenderloin,
    cut in $^1/_2$-inch dice
$^1/_2$ cup olive oil
1 yellow onion, diced
1 red bell pepper, diced
$^1/_2$ cup diced tomato
1 cup chopped ham
6 cloves garlic, minced

2 cups short-grain Calasparra rice
pinch of saffron
2 teaspoons smoked paprika
1 tablespoon thyme
6 cups Chicken Stock (page 37)
salt and pepper to taste
4 cups fresh spinach, cleaned
    and chopped

In a large skillet or paella pan, brown the pork in half of the olive oil. Remove from pan and set aside.

Sauté the onion, bell pepper, tomato, ham, and garlic in the pork fat and the remainder of the olive oil until the onions are soft. Add the rice and sauté until coated with oil. Add the saffron, paprika, and thyme.

Add 3 cups of the Chicken Stock and bring to a simmer; cook for 5 to 7 minutes. Add salt and pepper. Add the cooked pork, spinach, and remainder of the Chicken Stock. Try not to stir any more at this point, but don't let the rice stick to the bottom of the pan too much either. Stick your spoon into the pan and check to see if anything is sticking on the bottom; stir only if you have to.

Keep on medium-low heat until the rice is cooked, about 15 minutes. Turn off the heat and allow to rest for 5 to 10 minutes; serve.

# Paella Mixta
*Poultry and Seafood Rice Dish*

*Spanish cuisine, like the culture, is a complex mosaic of various influences, and paella is the dish that best resembles this multicultural fusion. It is a bold ambrosia of seemingly unrelated parts incorporating grains, flowers, vegetables, meat, fish, and fowl. Paella has become the quintessential dish of Spanish cuisine.*

*Paella is surprisingly quick and easy to make. You must follow the cooking procedures in a specific order because the main ingredients all have different cooking times. Paella Mixta is a good basic paella that can be made at home with ingredients that are fairly easy to find.*

MAKES 4 SERVINGS

4 chicken legs
$^1/_2$ cup olive oil
2 links dry chorizo, 1 diced and 1 sliced
1 yellow onion, diced
1 tablespoon minced garlic
2 cups short-grain Calasparra rice
2 pinches saffron
$2^1/_2$ cups Fish Stock (page 39) or clam juice
$2^1/_3$ cups Chicken Stock (page 37)
salt and pepper to taste
$^1/_2$ cup diced tomato
$^1/_2$ cup diced red bell pepper
$^1/_2$ cup green peas
8 littleneck clams
8 black mussels
8 large shrimp, peeled
2 small lobsters or 8 crawfish, shelled

Make the paella on the stovetop in a large skillet or paella pan without a lid. In the pan, cook the chicken in half of the olive oil until cooked through. Remove from pan and set aside. Set *sliced* chorizo aside.

In the same pan using the chicken fat and the rest of the olive oil, sauté onion and *diced* chorizo until onion is soft. Add the garlic. Add the rice and stir until each grain is coated with oil. Add the saffron.

Combine Fish Stock or clam juice with Chicken Stock to make cooking liquid. Add 3 cups of the cooking liquid to the pan and bring to a simmer. Cook for about 5 to 7 minutes. Add salt and pepper. Then add the tomato, bell pepper, and peas. Stir.

As you add the rest of the ingredients, use more cooking liquid as needed. Try not to stir any more at this point, but don't let the rice stick to the bottom of the pan too much. Stick your spoon into the pan and check to see if any thing is sticking on the bottom; stir only if you have to.

Add clams by pushing them down into the rice. Wait 3 to 4 minutes, then add the mussels. Add more liquid.

Add *sliced* chorizo, cooked chicken legs, shrimp, and lobster or crawfish meat in that order. Add more liquid if needed.

When lobster and shrimp meat are cooked (they will turn pink after about 2 minutes), it is done. Serve with slices of rustic bread and a hearty Spanish or Argentine wine.  ❧

Paella Mixta

# Paella de Gambas y Morcilla

*Shrimp and Blood Sausage Rice Dish*

*I like the balance of the richness of the blood sausage against the brininess of the shrimp and fish stock in this dish. The blood sausage will fall apart and become a flavorful paste that mixes with the rice for a deep color and complex flavor.*

MAKES 4 SERVINGS

1 yellow onion, diced
$^1/_2$ cup diced tomato
$^3/_4$ cup olive oil
4 cloves garlic, minced
$^1/_2$ pound chorizo, diced
$^1/_2$ pound morcilla (blood sausage), diced
pinch of saffron
1 teaspoon smoked paprika
2 cups short-grain Calasparra rice
6 cups Fish Stock (page 39)
$^1/_2$ cup fino sherry
salt and pepper
1 pound fresh shrimp, peeled and deveined
grated peel of 1 lemon

In a large skillet or paella pan, sauté the onion and tomato in the olive oil. Add the garlic.

Add the chorizo and morcilla and cook on medium-high heat for 4 to 5 minutes while stirring. Add the saffron and paprika. Stir. Add the rice and sauté until coated with oil. Add half of the Fish Stock and bring to a simmer for 5 to 7 minutes. Then add the rest of the stock and bring to a boil. Add the fino and salt and pepper.

Cook on medium-low heat for about 12 minutes, then stir in the shrimp and lemon peel. Cook another 3 to 5 minutes, until rice is tender. Then serve.

**Pepita-Crusted Salmon with
Toasted Cumin Tomato Sauce**

# Pepita-Crusted Salmon with Toasted Cumin Tomato Sauce

*Crunchy toasted green pumpkin seeds (pepitas) give a nice balance to the fleshy, smooth texture of the salmon in this recipe.*

MAKES 4 SERVINGS

2 pounds salmon fillet
$1/_2$ cup olive oil
3 tablespoons fresh lime juice
$1^1/_4$ cups pepitas
1 tablespoon coriander seeds
1 teaspoon salt
$1/_2$ teaspoon cracked black pepper
1 teaspoon garlic powder
12 ounces Toasted Cumin Tomato Sauce (page 27)

Cut salmon fillet into 4 (8-ounce) pieces. Coat fish with $1/_4$ cup olive oil and the lime juice. Refrigerate for 1 to 2 hours. Preheat the oven to 375 degrees.

Toast pepitas in a hot, dry skillet until they brown and pop (puff up). Set aside to cool. Toast the coriander seeds until brown and lightly smoking. Set aside to cool. When cool, crush the coriander in a spice grinder. Put the pepitas in a food processor and process while adding the coriander, salt, pepper, and garlic powder. Rub the pepita mixture on both sides of the salmon.

Heat the remaining olive oil in a large skillet; cook the salmon fillets for about two minutes per side, then transfer the pan to the oven. Cook for 12 to 14 minutes. Heat the Toasted Cumin Tomato Sauce and have 4 plates ready. Pour about 3 ounces of sauce on each plate and place the salmon on top of the sauce to serve. ✑

# Trout Wrapped in Jamon Serrano

*This simple dish is seared with a little olive oil so that the ham gets nice and crispy.*

MAKES 4 SERVINGS

4 thin slices of jamon serrano
4 (6-ounce) trout fillets
$^1/_2$ cup olive oil
2 tablespoons grated lemon peel
2 tablespoons minced garlic
2 tablespoons chopped fresh mint
1 teaspoon salt
$^1/_2$ teaspoon cracked black pepper

Cut 4 slices of jamon serrano, about 6 inches long and 2 inches wide. Coat the fish with $^1/_4$ cup of olive oil. Mix the lemon peel, garlic, mint, salt, and pepper, and rub on the trout. Wrap each piece of trout with a slice of jamon. Heat a large skillet or flat grill with the remaining olive oil and sear the fish (skin-side-up first) for about 1 minute on medium heat. Turn over and cook for another 2 minutes. Turn the heat down to low and cook for another minute or so. Transfer to plates and serve with Orange-Fennel-Olive Salad (page 76) and Lemon-Caper Aioli (page 5).

# Zarzuela de Mariscos
*Operetta of Shellfish*

*The name alone inspires a cook to make this stew sing!*

MAKES 4 SERVINGS

1 cup olive oil
10 cloves garlic
1 cup Migas (page 34)
$^1/_2$ cup Marcona almonds, roasted
$^1/_4$ cup chopped parsley
1 cup Sofrito (page 3)
$^1/_2$ cup amontillado sherry
6 cups Fish Stock (page 39)

1 pound fresh black mussels
1 pound fresh clams
1 pound large shrimp, peeled and
    deveined
$^1/_2$ pound bay scallops, shelled
pinch of saffron
1 tablespoon sweet smoked paprika
cracked black pepper to taste

Heat the olive oil in a small saucepan and add the cloves of garlic; fry until dark brown. Remove from the heat and let stand 15 minutes. This will allow the garlic to fully cook while flavoring the oil. Remove the garlic with a slotted spoon and transfer to a mortar and pestle. Reserve the garlic oil. Crush the garlic with the mortar and pestle along with the Migas, almonds, and parsley. Set this mixture aside. It will serve as a flavorful thickener for the stew.

Heat the Sofrito in a deep skillet and add a few tablespoons of the garlic oil. Deglaze the pan with the sherry. Add the Fish Stock, mussels, clams, shrimp, scallops, saffron, and paprika. Cover and cook on high heat until the mussels and clams pop open. Stir in the almond-garlic mixture and cook on low heat for a few more minutes, then add the black pepper and taste. Adjust seasoning, adding salt if needed. Serve in bowls and drizzle with remaining garlic oil.

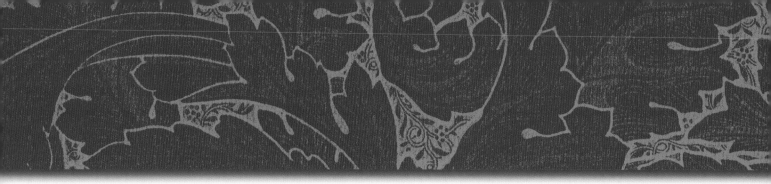

# Puerco con Manzanas y Cabrales

Pork Tenderloin with Apples and Cabrales Cheese

*Chilled pork tenderloin with apples and Cabrales blue cheese is a cold entrée great for a summer lunch or light dinner.*

MAKES 4 ENTRÉE SERVINGS

2 whole pork tenderloins
salt and pepper
2 Granny Smith apples, cored, cut in
    half, and sliced into thin wedges
$^1/_2$ cup crumbled Cabrales cheese (or
    other blue cheese)

**For Marinade:**
$^1/_2$ cup tomato juice
3 tablespoons minced garlic
1 tablespoon fresh thyme leaves
$^1/_4$ cup brown sugar
1 bay leaf
2 tablespoons sherry vinegar
$^1/_2$ cup olive oil
1 teaspoon whole cloves

Combine all ingredients for the marinade and mix well. Pour over pork tenderloins. Cover pork and refrigerate for at least 4 hours, or overnight if you have time.

Preheat oven to 375 degrees. Remove pork from marinade and sprinkle with salt and pepper. Place on a baking pan and roast for about 15 minutes. Allow to cool to room temperature, then refrigerate for 1 hour. Slice pork loins into about 24 thin medallions. Put 6 slices on each plate along with 6 apple slices. Top each serving with crumbled Cabrales and serve. Optional serving suggestion: Drizzle with Vinagre de Jerez (page 17).

Puerco con Manzanas y Cabrales

# Beef Tenderloin with Cabrales Butter

MAKES 4 ENTRÉE SERVINGS

24 ounces beef tenderloin
4 tablespoons minced garlic
3 tablespoons chopped fresh rosemary
$1/4$ cup olive oil
2 tablespoons salt
1 tablespoon cracked black pepper
3 tablespoons balsamic vinegar
Cabrales Butter (page 11) for garnish

Stir together all ingredients except beef and Cabrales Butter. Rub mixture on beef; wrap in plastic and refrigerate for 24 hours. Preheat oven to 375 degrees. In a hot cast-iron skillet, sear the tenderloin on all sides. Transfer to the oven and cook for about 15 to 20 minutes for medium rare. Remove from oven and allow the meat to rest for 5 minutes before cutting. Cut the tenderloin into 4 thick steaks and serve with 2 tablespoons of melted Cabrales Butter on each plate. ❧

# Rabo de Toro

*Braised Oxtail*

Oxtail is a hearty treat for many Mediterranean and Latin American people. In Mexico it is called "cola de la baca," and its succulent fatty meat makes a great taco filling. In Texas they affectionately call it "swingin' steak." Oxtail can produce some of the tastiest broth you've ever had. It's great for adding to beef bones when making stock and will add a rich, velvety texture to the finished product.

Oxtail is not expensive, exotic, or hard to find. You can find it in most grocery stores; I think many people simply do not know what it is or how it should be cooked. It has the appearance of veal or lamb shank, only smaller.

This recipe has some definite Mexican accents of canela and ancho chile, but it is made with a very Provençal French technique. Try it if you are looking for something different on a cold winter night or an excuse to open a nice, hearty bottle of red wine.

MAKES 4 SERVINGS

8 pounds oxtail, cut in 2-inch sections and trimmed of excess fat
$3/_4$ cup flour
salt and black pepper to taste
$1/_4$ cup olive oil
$1/_2$ cup diced carrots
$1/_2$ cup diced celery
$1/_2$ white onion, diced

4 cups red wine
6 quarts beef stock
2 tablespoons minced garlic
2 sprigs fresh thyme
2 tablespoons tomato paste
3 bay leaves
3 sticks of canela or cinnamon
2 dried ancho chiles

Preheat oven to 325 degrees. Sprinkle the oxtail with flour (enough to coat) and salt and pepper. Heat olive oil on the stove in a large, deep skillet on high heat. Add the oxtail and brown on all sides. Remove and set aside.

Add carrots, celery, and onion to the pan and sauté in the fat until soft. Put the oxtail back into the pan, and add the red wine. Deglaze the pan, scraping up the small flavorful bits that may be sticking to the bottom. Cook over medium heat until wine thickens a bit, then add remaining ingredients. Bring to a boil. Cover the pan and put it in the oven for $3^1/_2$ hours. Remove from the oven and serve 2 to 3 pieces of oxtail over cooked pasta or roasted potatoes. Spoon the juices and vegetables over the meat. ❧

Roasted Duck with
Moroccan Carrot Sauce

# Roasted Duck with Moroccan Carrot Sauce

*The sweetness of cooked carrots with aromas of cumin and cinnamon cause this dish to get rave reviews every time.*

MAKES 4 ENTRÉE SERVINGS

1 whole duckling

**For Marinade:**
2 whole oranges, cut into fourths
$^1/_4$ cup soy sauce
10 cloves garlic
3 tablespoons brown sugar
$^1/_4$ cup chopped fresh Italian parsley
1 white onion
2 bay leaves
2 stalks of celery, chopped
1 whole jalapeño pepper, stem removed

Put all ingredients for the marinade in a food processor and puree well. Rub on the duck. Refrigerate for at least 4 hours. Preheat oven to 400 degrees and roast duck for 1 hour in an uncovered roasting pan. Serve with warm Moroccan Carrot Sauce (page 21) and Mediterranean Couscous Salad (page 67).

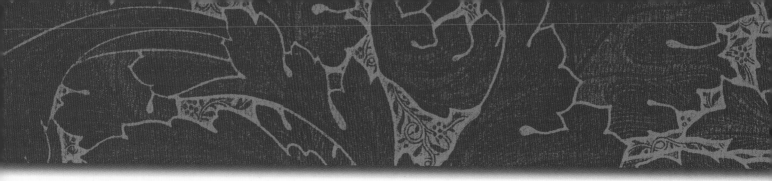

# Cordero Harissa

*Lamb with Harissa*

*These marinated whole lamb racks are roasted and served with exotic, spicy Tunisian Harissa sauce.*

2 whole lamb racks, trimmed of excess fat

**For Marinade:**
2 tablespoons fennel seed
1 tablespoon sherry vinegar
3 tablespoons orange zest
$1/4$ cup chopped fresh mint
$1/4$ cup chopped fresh cilantro
6 cloves garlic
$1/4$ cup molasses
1 yellow onion, peeled and chopped

Combine all marinade ingredients in a food processor until a smooth, thick paste is formed. Rub on lamb racks on all sides. Refrigerate for 24 hours.

Preheat oven to 375 degrees. Roast lamb in an uncovered pan for 30 to 40 minutes. Cut into chops and serve with lots of Harissa Sauce (page 24) and Rosemary-Yogurt Flatbread (page 123). ❧

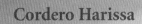
Cordero Harissa

# Cod with Clams and Chorizo

*This dish is a nice seafood-pork combination of Spanish origin.*

1 cup chopped yellow onion

$^{1}/_{4}$ cup shredded carrots

4 tablespoons minced garlic

$^{1}/_{4}$ cup olive oil

$^{1}/_{2}$ cup chopped chorizo

$1^{1}/_{2}$ pounds fresh cod, cut into 4 pieces

1 pound fresh clams

$^{1}/_{2}$ cup chopped parsley

1 roma tomato, diced

1 tablespoon chopped fresh oregano

1 cup clam juice

1 cup Manzanilla sherry

2 tablespoons butter

In a large skillet, sauté the onion, carrots, and garlic in olive oil until soft. Add the chorizo and sauté for another 2 to 3 minutes. Add the remaining ingredients and cover. Turn to medium-high heat and cook for about 7 minutes. Divide evenly into bowls and serve with good bread. For a heartier version, pour over Mediterranean Couscous Salad (page 67).

# Carne Milanesa with Lemon-Caper Aioli

*Breaded Beef Cutlets with Lemon-Caper Mayonnaise*

*You may need to make a double batch; these tend to get eaten as fast as they come out of the pan!*

MAKES 4 ENTRÉE SERVINGS

12 ounces beef tenderloin

2 cups flour

6 eggs

$1^1/_2$ teaspoons salt

$1^1/_2$ teaspoons cracked black pepper

2 cups bread crumbs

$^1/_4$ cup grated Parmesan cheese

2 tablespoons chopped parsley

$^1/_4$ cup olive oil

Cut the beef into 4 (3-ounce) pieces and pound each piece to about a $^1/_2$-inch thickness. Put the flour in a shallow bowl or on a plate. In a separate bowl, beat the eggs with the salt and the pepper. In another bowl, mix the bread crumbs with the cheese and parsley.

Bread the meat by dredging in flour, then egg, then bread crumbs (in that order). Heat a cast-iron skillet with the olive oil and fry the cutlets 1 or 2 at a time on medium heat for about 1 minute per side. Transfer to plates and serve with Lemon-Caper Aioli (page 5) and Tortilla Española (page 79).

Grilled Quail with
Espresso-Chipotle Sauce

# Grilled Quail with Espresso-Chipotle Sauce

*If you can find semi-boneless quail, eating these flavorful little birds will be a little easier. The Espresso-Chipotle Sauce can also be used on duck, pheasant, or chicken.*

MAKES 8 SERVINGS

8 whole quail, semi-boneless if possible
3 cups Espresso-Chipotle Sauce (page 22)

**For Marinade:**
10 cloves garlic
1 tablespoon chopped fresh rosemary
$1/_2$ teaspoon ground allspice
2 tablespoons sherry vinegar
$1/_2$ cup olive oil
1 tablespoon salt

Combine all marinade ingredients. Add quail and marinate for 4 to 5 hours. Light a charcoal or gas grill. Grill the quail on medium heat for about 4 minutes per side. In the meantime, bring Espresso-Chipotle Sauce to a boil on the stove in a large, round sauté pan. Transfer the quail to the pan of hot sauce to finish cooking . Turn down to medium heat and cook for about 7 minutes while spooning the sauce over the quail. Serve over rice or with Patatas Bravas (page 129). ✎

# Grilled Lobster with Chipotle-Mustard Vinaigrette

*This is a nice summertime meal served with some cold sides such as Orange-Fennel-Olive Salad (page 76) and Marinated Peruvian Purple Potatoes (page 70).*

MAKES 4 SERVINGS

2 tablespoons sea salt
4 whole live Maine lobsters
$^1/_4$ cup olive oil
1 cup Chipotle-Mustard Vinaigrette (page 16)

In a large pot, bring $1^1/_2$ gallons of water and the salt to a boil. Submerge lobsters, head first in the boiling water. Bring the water back to a boil and cook for about 3 minutes. Remove lobsters with tongs and submerge in ice water. At this point they will be partially cooked; they will cook fully on the grill.

Prepare a hot charcoal or gas grill. Split the lobsters in half lengthwise and leave in the shell. Remove stomach sac and other internal organs. Brush meat side with olive oil and vinaigrette; grill shell-side up for 2 to 3 minutes. Flip over and grill for 1 more minute until meat looks white and tender. Brush with more vinaigrette if you like. Serve immediately. ❧

# Postres

# Chocolate al Vapor

*Steamed Chocolate Cake*

*These moist cakes are cooked in individual baking cups or ramekins and served warm with fresh whipped cream.*

MAKES 6 SERVINGS

$^1/_2$ cup water
6 ounces unsweetened chocolate
1 cup butter
6 egg yolks
$1^1/_2$ cups sugar
seeds of 1 vanilla bean
2 teaspoons ground canela or cinnamon
$^1/_4$ cup flour
6 egg whites
pinch of salt

Heat the water; melt the chocolate by stirring it into the hot water. Stir in the butter, yolks, sugar, vanilla bean seeds, cinnamon, and flour until smooth. Whip egg whites with salt; gently fold into chocolate mixture. Pour into 6 (4-ounce) baking cups that have been sprayed with vegetable oil. Bake at 350 degrees in 2 inches of water for 30 minutes. Allow to cool for 5 minutes. Unmold and serve warm with fresh whipped cream. ❧

# Higos y Datiles

*Mascarpone-Stuffed Figs and Dates*

*Mascarpone-stuffed figs and dates with pistachios, oranges, and Pedro Ximenez Caramel Sauce. These basic Mediterranean flavors make a near-perfect flavor combination when taken together in one bite. Serve as a dessert or cheese course.*

MAKES 4 SERVINGS

12 large dried figs

12 large pitted dates

$^1/_2$ cup Mascarpone cheese

20 orange sections

$^1/_2$ cup shelled pistachios, lightly toasted and crushed

$^1/_2$ cup Pedro Ximenez Caramel Sauce (page 172)

Slice each fig and date lengthwise without cutting all the way through and press them open. Fill each fig and date with Mascarpone cheese. Arrange 3 filled figs and 3 filled dates on each plate. Top with orange sections and pistachios; drizzle with caramel sauce. ◕

Higos y Datiles

# El Farol Goat Cheese Tart

*A simple, sweet goat cheese tart that resembles a thin cheesecake.*

MAKES 2 (9-INCH) TARTS

**For Tart Shells:**

1 cup plus 1 tablespoon confectioners' sugar

1³/₄ cups all-purpose flour

pinch of salt

8 tablespoons unsalted butter, softened

1 egg

**For Filling:**

¹/₂ pound soft, fresh Spanish or domestic goat cheese

¹/₂ cup honey

2 eggs

2 teaspoons ground anise

1 tablespoon finely chopped fresh rosemary

1 teaspoon ground cinnamon

2 tablespoons grated lemon peel

1 tablespoon grated orange peel

To Make Tart Shells:

Sift together the confectioners' sugar, flour, and salt in a medium bowl. Place the butter in the bowl of a food processor and process until smooth, about 15 seconds. Scatter the flour mixture over the butter, add the egg, and process just until the dough starts to come together in a ball. Do not overmix. Put the dough onto the counter and divide it in two. Shape each half into a disc, wrap in plastic wrap, and refrigerate for at least 2 hours or up to 24 hours.

Let the dough stand at room temperature for 30 minutes to soften. Lightly butter two 9-inch fluted tart pans with removable bottoms. Dust a work surface lightly with flour. Dust one of the discs lightly with flour and, using a floured rolling pin, roll it out into a rough 12-inch circle. Roll up the dough onto the rolling pin and gently unroll it over one of the prepared tart pans. Press the dough into the pan and roll the pin over the top of the pan to remove the excess dough. Repeat with the remaining dough and tart pan. Prick the bottom of the tart shells all over with a fork. Chill the tart shells for 20 minutes in the refrigerator. The tart shells can be refrigerated for up to 24 hours.

Preheat the oven to 325 degrees. Lightly butter two pieces of aluminum foil large enough to generously line each tart pan. Line the tart shells with the foil, buttered-side-down, and fill with dried beans, rice, or pie weights. Bake the tart shells for 15 minutes. Remove the foil and beans and continue baking for 8 to 10 minutes longer, until evenly golden brown. Cool completely on a wire rack.

To Make Filling:
Beat goat cheese and honey together until smooth. Mix in other ingredients. Fill prebaked tart shells and bake at 350 degrees for 25 minutes or until set. ◡

# Lemon-Rosemary Flan

*Our biggest-selling dessert is a classic with some surprising flavor combinations.*

MAKES 6 (4-OUNCE) FLANS

**For Caramel:**
1$\frac{1}{2}$ cups white sugar
$\frac{1}{4}$ cup water

**For Custard:**
2 cups heavy cream
2 sprigs fresh rosemary
rind of 1 lemon
1 vanilla bean, split
$\frac{1}{2}$ cup sugar
2 whole eggs
2 egg yolks

Preheat oven to 300 degrees. To make the caramel, put the sugar and the water in a saucepan over low to medium heat until melted and a light amber color. Pour a little caramel syrup into 6 (4-ounce) ramekins.

To make the custard, heat the heavy cream with the rosemary, lemon rind, and vanilla bean until bubbling. Stir in the sugar and remove from heat; let rest for 10 minutes. This will allow the lemon and rosemary flavors to infuse in the hot cream. Strain. Beat the eggs and yolks together. Add a little hot cream to the eggs and whisk together. Then add a little more cream to the eggs; this will temper the eggs. Now whisk the egg mixture into the cream. Fill each ramekin with the custard mixture and bake in a water bath for about 30 minutes. Allow to cool to room temperature and then chill for 1 hour before serving. Unmold on a plate and drizzle the caramel syrup around the custard.

Lemon-Rosemary Flan

# Pastelitos de Dulce de Membrillo

*Fried Pastry Filled with Quince Paste*

*This is an unusual dessert or after-noon pastry filled with membrillo and Manchego cheese.*

MAKES 12 SMALL PASTRIES

1 batch empanada dough (page 91)
1 egg beaten and mixed with 2 tablespoons water, for egg wash
12 pieces of membrillo, sliced $1/_2$-inch thick in 2-inch squares
12 slices of Manchego cheese $1/_4$-inch thick in 2-inch squares
1 quart vegetable oil for frying
powdered sugar
$1/_2$ cup crushed Marcona almonds

Roll out the dough very thin (about $1/_8$-inch thick) on a floured surface. Cut 24 (3-inch) squares. Lay out 12 squares of dough and brush the edges with the egg wash. Top each with a piece of membrillo and a piece of Manchego. Place the remaining 12 pieces of dough on top of the cheese to form a ravioli shape. Crimp the edges together with your fingers or with a fork. Heat the oil to about 350 degrees and deep-fry pastries 4 at a time, until golden brown, about 1 minute. Remove from oil and place on a plate lined with paper towels. Sprinkle liberally with powdered sugar and crushed almonds. Serve with good strong coffee or Pedro Ximenez sherry.  ❧

# Lavender Goat's Milk Flan

*The goat's milk makes surprisingly smooth and luxurious custard.*

MAKES 6 (4-OUNCE) SERVINGS

**For Caramel:**
1 cup white sugar
$^1/_4$ cup water
$^1/_2$ cup honey

**For Custard:**
1 cup goat's milk
$^1/_2$ cup dry lavender or $^1/_4$ cup fresh lavender
$^1/_2$ cup sugar
2 whole eggs
2 egg yolks
fresh lavender sprigs for garnish

Preheat oven to 300 degrees. Melt the sugar in a saucepan with the water on low to medium heat until an amber brown, then stir in the honey. Pour a little of this syrup into each of the 6 ramekins.

To make the custard, heat the milk with the lavender until bubbling. Stir in the sugar and remove from the heat. Allow to stand for about 10 minutes, then strain. Beat the eggs and egg yolks together. Pour a little hot milk into the egg mixture and whisk together. Add a little more milk. Now whisk the egg mixture into the milk. Fill each ramekin with the custard mixture and bake in a water bath for about 30 minutes. Allow to cool to room temperature and then chill for at least 1 hour before serving. Unmold on a plate and serve with a sprig of fresh lavender. ✑

# Orange Polenta Almond Cake

*This very rustic cake uses whole oranges, peel and all, to maximize the citrus flavor.*

MAKES 2 (8-INCH) CAKES

1$^1/_2$ quarts water
2 whole oranges, with peel
1 cup flour
2 tablespoons cornstarch
1 cup polenta
1$^1/_2$ cups Marcona almonds, roasted
1$^1/_2$ cups butter
2 cups sugar
6 eggs
1 teaspoon Mexican vanilla extract

Boil water and simmer the whole oranges for about 30 minutes. Remove and let cool. In a mixing bowl, place all dry ingredients except almonds. Grind almonds until smooth. Add to dry ingredients and mix well. Set aside.

Process the oranges in a food processor. Cream butter and sugar. Add eggs, slowly, 1 at a time. Add orange puree and vanilla. Add dry ingredients and beat until combined. Cook in buttered 8-inch cake pans for about 40 minutes at 325 degrees. Serve with Port-Fig Syrup (page 26).

# Raspado de Sangria

*Citrus-Wine-Flavored Ice*

*This is a frozen ice granita made with our famous sangria. You will need to freeze this mixture and then scrape with the edge of a large spoon to make a soft shaved ice.*

MAKES 10 TO 12 SERVINGS

2 cups water
1 cup sugar
2 cups red or white sangria (pages 179, 180)
6 ounces orange juice concentrate

Bring the water to a boil and remove from heat. Stir in the sugar until dissolved, then stir in the sangria and the orange juice concentrate. Pour into a shallow metal or plastic container and allow to cool to room temperature. Cover and freeze. Stir the mixture every 20 minutes for the first $1^1/_2$ hours. When completely frozen, scrape with the side of a large spoon. Scoop into wineglasses and serve with fresh orange sections for a light, cool dessert or palate cleanser. ❧

# Torrijas
## Sugared Cocoa Toasts

*This is rustic peasant cooking at its best. Just when it seems you have nothing on hand for a quick snack or dessert, you could whip out some torrijas made from leftover bread and a few pantry ingredients. Try these with morning coffee and start your day off right.*

MAKES 4 SERVINGS

$^1/_4$ cup powdered sugar

2 tablespoons cocoa powder

1 tablespoon ground cinnamon

$^1/_2$ cup milk

2 eggs, beaten

8 baguette slices, 1 inch thick

$^1/_4$ cup vegetable oil

1 tablespoon butter

Mix sugar, cocoa, and cinnamon; set aside. Stir the milk into the beaten eggs. Soak the bread in this mixture for 1 minute, making sure both sides soak up some liquid. Heat oil and butter together in a skillet and fry the bread for about 30 seconds per side. Remove from pan and sprinkle liberally with sugar mixture while still hot. ❧

# Sweet Coconut Rice Pudding

MAKES **8** SERVINGS

3 cups whole milk

$3^1/_2$ cups coconut milk, unsweetened

2 sticks canela or cinnamon

3 strips lemon rind

pinch of salt

$^3/_4$ cup white rice

1 tablespoon ground anise seed

$^1/_2$ cup white sugar

1 teaspoon Mexican vanilla extract

$^1/_2$ teaspoon almond extract

orange slices, shredded coconut, and shaved almonds for garnish

In a large saucepan, combine whole milk with coconut milk and bring to a boil with the canela and lemon rind. Add salt, rice, anise, and sugar. Stir. Add vanilla and almond extracts. Cook uncovered at low heat for about 1 hour, stirring occasionally. Remove canela and lemon rind. Divide into serving dishes and chill. Garnish with orange slices, shredded coconut, and shaved almonds.  ❧

Torta de Chocolate

# Torta de Chocolate

*Double Chocolate-Espresso Flourless Torte*

*Caution chocolate lovers! This deep, rich chocolaty experience may be addictive. Canela provides some lively new-world punch to the mix of flavors.*

MAKES 1 (9-INCH) CAKE

2 tablespoons vegetable oil

1 cup strong espresso (liquid, not beans), or 1 cup of boiling water
   with 1$^{1}/_{2}$ tablespoons instant espresso powder dissolved in it

2 cups butter, unsalted

1$^{1}/_{2}$ cups packed brown sugar

16 ounces unsweetened chocolate

zest of one lemon, chopped

2 teaspoons ground canela or cinnamon

8 eggs

whipped cream for garnish

Preheat the oven to 350 degrees. Oil the inside bottom and sides of a springform pan and line bottom with parchment paper. Put espresso, butter, and sugar in a small saucepan and bring to a boil. Have chocolate ready in a large mixing bowl. Remove espresso mixture from heat and stir in the zest and the canela. Pour this mixture over the chocolate to melt it and whisk together. Beat the eggs, then whisk into the chocolate mixture. Fill the pan with the mixture and bake for about 40 minutes. Cool to room temperature, then refrigerate for at least 1 hour. Release from pan and serve in wedges with whipped cream. ∾

# Pedro Ximenez Caramel Sauce

*Pedro Ximenez is a sweet and figgy sherry from Spain. Other sweet sherries may be used as a substitute. Pour over gelato, ice cream, crepes, or fried bananas.*

MAKES 1 CUP

$^1/_2$ cup butter
$^1/_2$ cup brown sugar
$^1/_4$ cup heavy cream
$^1/_4$ cup Pedro Ximenez sherry

Cut butter into small pieces and melt in a saucepan. Stir in sugar and cream. Cook over low heat, whisking until everything is melted and blended, about 2 minutes. Stir in the sherry. Serve warm. ❧

# Milagro Sugar Cookies

Milagros, or "miracles," are symbols of various body parts, people, animals, and even automobiles. These symbols, usually small and made of metal, aid in focusing prayer on a particular problem. Milagros nailed onto black wooden crosses have become a religious and folk art tradition in Spain, Italy, and Mexico. There are no special cookie cutters for these miraculous treats, so you will need to find pictures or some real milagros in order to copy the designs and cut the cookies freehand. Frost with Royal Icing (page 174).

MAKES ABOUT 3 DOZEN 4-INCH COOKIES

3 cups flour
$1/_2$ teaspoon baking soda
1 teaspoon salt
1 teaspoon ground canela or cinnamon
1 cup butter
1 cup sugar
2 eggs
1 tablespoon Mexican vanilla

Preheat oven to 375 degrees. Mix flour, baking soda, salt, and canela in a bowl; set aside. In the bowl of an electric mixer, cream together the butter and sugar. Beat for 30 seconds. Add eggs and vanilla. Then add the dry ingredients. Mix well until a dough forms with all ingredients well incorporated.

Roll out the dough on a floured surface to about $1/_8$-inch thickness and cut out *milagro* shapes. Transfer shapes to a lightly greased cookie sheet and bake for about 10 to 12 minutes. Allow to cool before decorating. ❧

# Royal Icing

Real milagros are made of metal, so frosting the cookies with some kind of silver or gray-colored icing will imitate that look. A good craft shop will have cake-decorating supplies. You will need an edible silver powder or glitter to incorporate into the icing recipe. If you cannot find this, you may have to mix food colorings until you get a silvery gray. This recipe is a standard "Royal Icing" made from egg whites, which sets up hard and sturdy.

MAKES ABOUT 2 CUPS OF ICING

2 egg whites
3 cups powdered sugar
1 tablespoon lemon juice
$1/4$ teaspoon salt
approximately $1/2$ teaspoon silver or gray coloring

Combine all ingredients in an electric mixer and beat well for 2 to 3 minutes, or until the mixture holds peaks. Adjust color to your liking. Apply a thin layer to each cookie, enough to completely cover the top and edges. ❧

# Drinks

# Nectar de los Dioses

*Nectar of the Gods!*

*Gifts from Mexico are endless in Santa Fe, but tequila is one of the most prized. I didn't think tequila could be improved upon until I tasted this concoction from our bar manager, Warren MacNaughton. The tequila is infused with tropical fruits and allowed to rest and develop flavor for at least one week.*

MAKES 12 TO 15 SERVINGS

$^1/_4$ pineapple, peeled
$^1/_2$ fresh papaya, peeled
$^1/_2$ fresh mango, peeled
$^1/_4$ honeydew melon, peeled
$^1/_2$ cantaloupe, peeled
1 vanilla bean, split
1 stick of canela or cinnamon
1 bottle Cuervo Traditional Tequila
2 tablespoons brown sugar

Place peeled fruit, vanilla bean, and canela in a large glass container. Mix tequila with the sugar and pour over the fruit. Cover and set aside at room temperature for 7 days. Serve straight up or on the rocks.  ❧

Sangria Tinta de El Farol

# Sangria Tinta de El Farol
*Red Sangria*

This is a crowd-pleasing blend
of fruit juices, wines, spices, and
brandy. Bring a chilled jug of
sangria on your next picnic or
camping trip.

MAKES ABOUT **8** SERVINGS OVER ICE

1 bottle of Spanish red wine
6 ounces soda water
5 ounces simple syrup
$^1/_2$ cup gin
$^1/_2$ cup brandy
$^1/_2$ teaspoon ground cloves
1 teaspoon ground canela or cinnamon
juice of one orange
juice of one lime

Mix all the ingredients well and chill for at least 1 hour. Serve over ice with
citrus fruit wedges for garnish. ❧

To Make Simple Syrup:
Put 1 cup water in a small saucepan and add 2 cups sugar. Bring to a boil over
medium-high heat, stirring constantly. Reduce heat and continue to stir until
sugar is dissolved. Cool to room temperature.

Simple syrup can be stored in a sealed container in the refrigerator indefinitely.
Use whenever a recipe calls for simple sugar or simple syrup. Makes $1^1/_2$ cups.

# Sangria Blanca de El Farol
## White Sangria

*Here is a light, refreshing version of Sangria for those who prefer white wine.*

1 bottle Spanish white wine

$^1/_2$ cup cointreau

$^1/_2$ cup gin

6 ounces soda water

5 ounces simple syrup (page 179)

1 cup apple juice

one apple, peeled and quartered

juice of one orange

1 cup seedless white grapes for garnish

Mix all ingredients well and chill for at least 1 hour. Strain out the apple chunks. Serve over ice with white grapes for garnish. ౿

# Melon Mezcalito

*Mezcal Tequila with Melon*

*Wild, smoky flavors of mezcal tequila from Mexico are tamed and balanced well in this fruity favorite.*

MAKES 4 COCKTAILS

4 ounces mezcal

1 ounce citronage liqueur

1 ounce melon liquor

2 ounces fresh orange juice

2 ounces fresh lime juice

Mix well with ice and strain into four martini glasses. ❧

# Sangrita Oyster Shooters

*Can be served as a cold tapa or as a drink. This is a dish I developed for our annual Cinco de Mayo celebration. We have a five-course tequila tasting, and each tequila is presented with a tapa. Sangrita is a spicy tomato drink that often accompanies tequila in Mexico. Each raw oyster is served in a shot glass filled with sangrita. Pass the limes and salt and start shooting. Salud!*

MAKES 24 SHOOTERS

24 freshly shucked oysters
2 cups tomato juice
4 serrano chiles
juice of 2 limes
1/2 white onion, peeled and chopped
2 dashes of Cholula Hot Sauce
salt to taste

Shuck oysters and keep well chilled. For the sangrita, combine all other ingredients in a blender and puree well. Allow this mixture to chill for 1 hour. Put each oyster in a shot glass and cover each with sangrita. Serve chilled with salt, fresh lime wedges, and a good silver tequila. ❧

# Carajillo
*Brandy with Espresso and Sugar*

*This is a simple recipe for a traditional afternoon "pick me up."*

MAKES 1 SERVING

1 shot of strong espresso
$1/4$ ounce Spanish brandy
2 teaspoons turbinado (raw sugar)

Stir together in a small glass. Option: serve with steamed milk. ❧

# Siesta El Farol
*Tequila with Lime and Gin*

*Served under a shady portal in summer, this drink is custom-made for a lazy day.*

MAKES 4 SERVINGS

5 ounces Hornitos Tequila
3 ounces fresh lime juice
2 ounces sloe gin

Blend well over ice and strain into 4 chilled glasses.

# About Spanish Wines

**Albarino:** intense, aromatic white grape of high quality

**Anejo:** aged

**Cava:** sparkling wine

**Cosecha:** vintage

**Crianza:** aged a minimum of six months in oak and at least three years in the bottle before sale

**Garnacha:** full-bodied red grape

**Reserva:** minimum of twelve months in oak and not sold until four years after the harvest

**Gran Reserva:** minimum of twenty-four months in oak and not sold until six years after the harvest

**Tempranillo:** high quality, aromatic, predominant red grape in Spain

The ever-expanding El Farol wine cellar is 90 percent Spanish and 10 percent South American. We know that in Spain, living, breathing, eating, and drinking wine are all inseparable and essentially related activities. The wines have been designed to go with food since ancient times. With a wine-making tradition spanning more than 2,000 years, Spain is one of the oldest and most respected world-class wine producers in the world. They produce more wine than any other country on Earth and consume nearly 60 percent of this supply. So only about 10 percent makes it to the U.S.

Literally hundreds of different local grapes unique to the peninsula are harvested and used in endless varieties of combinations to produce quality and quantity of unusual proportions. There are as many as forty distinct wine regions in Spain and all of them produce excellent and unique products. Some of the best red wines in the world right now are coming out of the regions of Rioja, Ribera del Duero, and Penedes. Exciting whites such as Albarino with its lively gingery overtones and sparkling cavas are part of everyday life in Spain. Old and established techniques as well as modern adaptations that help consistency are at work here along with strict aging policies that give wines the time they need to fully develop in oak and in the bottle. It is difficult to find a bad Spanish wine because most of the producers are passionate about their art. But even with all of this history and passion, these wines are some of the best bargains on the shelves.

Here are some terms you should know when selecting a Spanish wine, but try to familiarize yourself by tasting as many different styles as you can. It won't cost much and you will definitely enjoy yourself more if you have a few tapas with your tasting. ❧

# Jerez
*Sherry*

**Amontillado:** after the *flordies* are off, the wine begins to oxidize, producing a light caramelization without being sweet. It is dry, nutty, and amber colored, served cold or room temperature.

**Fino:** fresh, dry, clean and served cold.

**Manzanilla:** a fino that is made next to the ocean, mostly in the fishing town of Sanlucar de Barrameda. Dry, briny, salty, and served cold.

**Oloroso:** complex, smooth, and aromatic. A rich brown color, dry and strong with a hint of fruit. Served room temperature.

**Palo Cortado:** a rare sherry that has characteristics of both amontillado and oloroso. Balanced, complex, and sometimes slightly sweet. It is served cold or at room temperature.

**Pedro Ximenez:** deep, aged sherry blended with sweet and raisin-like Pedro Ximenez grapes.

With all of the great Spanish wines available, the choices get more difficult when we consider drinking sherry with food. A true tapas experience must include at least a few types of sherry for maximum enjoyment. Vintages are aged in an ancient Roman solera system of pyramid-like stacks of barrels, and are blended for consistency, complexity, and history.

The sherries begin as simple white wines of the Palomino grape and are transformed into several varieties of noble and historically famous sherries. The wines range in style from fresh and briny, flavored by a layer of yeasty fungus called the *flor,* to swarthy and sweet, fortified with the rich and figgy Pedro Ximenez grape.

The subtle and distinctive Spanish flavors make sherries an important cooking wine and are used in many of our recipes. We highly recommend getting to know these wines from the southern-most regions of Spain and the towns of Jerez de la Frontera, Cadiz, and Sanlucar de Barrameda.

# Pantry Items

**Canela:** A soft stick, aromatic Ceylon cinnamon that is milder, more floral, and easier to crush than the hard cassia-type cinnamon usually found in the U.S. You can find this in most Hispanic markets.

**Capers and Caperberries:** Capers are handpicked pickled flower buds of a bush that grows in hot climates. Caper berries are the fruits of the same bush. These have the flavor of capers with a texture more like an olive.

**Cheeses:** The cheeses of Spain are some of the finest in the world. Many generations of artisans have been producing consistently superior products that are finally being discovered by American cooks. Again there are hundreds. I recommend sampling all that are available to you; you won't be disappointed. Here are a few:

*Cabrales:* This is a pungently tangy and rich blue cheese made from three milks; cow, sheep, and goat. It is difficult for me to use any other type of blue cheese in any recipe.

*Manchego:* The most famous Spanish cheese is this mild and nutty-flavored sheep's milk cheese. It is very versatile in cooking but a few slices with a glass of oloroso make a near perfect food and wine combination.

*Idiazabel:* A cheese made from fresh, unpasturized sheep's milk that is part of the history of the Basque shepherding tradition. Slightly sharp and smoky, it is excellent for grating on soups or pastas.

**Chipotle Chiles:** One of the very Mexican influences on our unique cuisine. These are red jalapeños that are dried and smoked over mesquite. They are very hot and spicy and when used properly offer a deep, complex smoky heat. You can find can *chipotles en adobo,* a hydrated form of the chile, in some supermarkets or Hispanic markets.

**Chorizo:** Spaniards are experts in the art of chartueturie. Pork products, especially sausages, are essential elements in the cuisine. There are literally hundreds of different types of chorizo. Most of these are simple mixtures of chopped pork meat and fat with garlic and smoked paprika (pimenton). We have a few favorites we like to keep on hand:

*Cantimpalo:* A mild-flavored, firm sausage for slicing and frying to serve as a tapa.

*Morcilla:* Rich and flavorful blood sausage with clove and paprika.

*Cantimpalitos:* Mini chorizo great for grilling on a skewer; one of our most popular dishes.

**Dulce de Membrillo:** Sweet and firm quince paste. It is usually sliced and paired with Manchego cheese. Excellent versions are produced in Mexico and Argentina as well as Spain. The Spanish products tend to be grainier and more flavorful.

**Jamon Serrano:** A mountain-air-cured ham from Spain, similar to prosciutto. Should be sliced very thin. A few slices on a small plate make an excellent tapa with sherry or white wine. Authentic imported hams are becoming more available each year.

**Marcona Almonds:** Simply the best almond anywhere. Round, flat, and incredibly rich tasting, these nuts are perfect for bold Spanish cooking, which calls for almonds more than any other cuisine. Fry in olive oil and toss with sea salt for a tapa.

**Pepitas:** Latin American green pumpkinseeds. Popular in Mexican markets, they are sold raw or toasted and salted. They have a nutty, earthy flavor that pairs well with cheeses and seafoods.

**Piquillo Peppers:** A mild red pepper from Spain, usually found canned or bottled. They are slowly and lightly smoked over wood fires, then peeled. Whole peppers can be stuffed and served as a cold tapa.

**Saffron:** Harvested stamen of the crocus flower. Adds distinct yellow color, floral aroma, and flavor to foods. This is notoriously expensive, but you only need very small amounts. There is a Latin American azafran that is the stamen of the safflower for a more earthy flavor and darker orange color. The flavor is much more rustic and not as fine as saffron.

**Smoked Paprika:** Pimenton is now available in many mainstream grocery stores. There are hot and sweet (mild) varieties that offer a unique smokiness to dishes.

# Sources

*The following three excellent online sources are recommended for food products and equipment.*

**The Santa Fe School of Cooking**

www.santafeschoolofcooking.com

Susan and Nicole Curtis offer cooking demonstrations by local and guest chefs. The online catalog features hard-to-find Mexican, New Mexican, Native American, and Latin American spices, products, cookbooks, and gift baskets.

**Tienda.com**

www.tienda.com

An excellent source for such Spanish food products as olives, Marcona almonds, cheeses, a wide variety of chorizos, and much more.

**The Spanish Table**

www.thespanishtable.hypermart.net

Specializing in such cooking products as paella pans, cazuelas, utensils, and other products from Spain and Portugal. The Spanish Table currently has three stores: Seattle, Berkeley, and Santa Fe.

# Index

**Numbers in boldface indicate a photograph.**

## A

Aioli: basic, 4; de garbanzos, 7; de higos, 6; lemon-caper, 5

Albarino, 189

Almond: -crusted seared tuna with toasted cumin tomato sauce, 85; chilled, garlic soup, 52; marcona, 196; orange polenta, cake, 166

Amontillado, 52, 191

Anejo, 189

Annatto, 118

Apples: in compota de manzanas y vino, 20; pork tenderloin with, and Cabrales cheese, 142, **143**

Arborio rice, 133

Artichokes, grilled, in saffron butter, 126, **127**

Avocado, crispy fried, **116**, 117

## B

Banana leaf, achiote citrus-steamed chicken in, 118

Bean, stew, Asturian white, 43

Beef: Argentine, empanadas, **90**, 91, **92**, 93; breaded, cutlets, 151; tenderloin with Cabrales butter, 144

Beets, roasted, 55

Bomba rice, 133

Brandy, 179, 184

Breads: fried, 34; pepita flatbread, 122; rosemary-yogurt flatbread, 123; sugared cocoa toasts, 168

Butter: beef tenderloin with Cabrales, 144; Cabrales, 10; green onion, 8; grilled artichokes in saffron, 126, **127**; preserved lemon, sauce, 13

## C

Cabrales, 195; butter, 10; beef tenderloin with, butter, 144; -stuffed fresh figs, 89; pork tenderloin with apples and, cheese, 142, **143**; portobello-, empanadas, **92**, 96–97

Cakes: double chocolate-espresso flourless torte, **170**, 171; orange polenta almond, 166; steamed chocolate, 157

Calamari, 114

Calasparra rice, 133

Caldo Pescado, **44**, 45

Canela, 195; in braised oxtail, 145; in double chocolate-espresso flourless torte, **170**, 171. *See also* Cinnamon

Cantimpalitos, 195

Cantimpalo, 195

Caperberries, 195

Caper(s), 195; grilled honey-, shrimp, **100**, 101; lemon-, aioli, 5

Caramel: with lavender goat's milk flan, 165; with lemon-rosemary flan, 162, **163**

Caramel Sauce, Pedro Ximenez, 172; Mascarpone-stuffed figs and dates with, 158, **159**

Carrot(s): Moroccan, sauce, 21; roasted duck with Moroccan, sauce, **146**, 147; steamed black mussels with, and jamon serrano in a Dijon-sherry cream sauce, **124**, 125

Catarina chile, jicama and lime with, 60

Cava, 189

Ceviche, 64; bay scallop, 65; salmon, with sweet corn vinaigrette, 66

Cheese(s): Cabrales-stuffed fresh figs, 89; definition of Spanish, 195; El Farol goat cheese tart, 160–61; in fried pastry filled with quince paste, 164; goat cheese and ham fritters, 106; goat cheese dressing, 61; grape salad with fresh mozzarella, **62**, 63; Manchego, 83, 164; Mascarpone-stuffed figs and dates, 158, **159;** pork tenderloin with apples and Cabrales, 142, **143;** portobello-Cabrales empanadas, **92,** 96–97; preserved lemon goat cheese spread, 72; queso fresco, 73

Chicken: achiote citrus-steamed, in banana leaf, 118; curried, salad with celery and grapes, 71; pollo harissa, 115; stock, 37

Chickpea: in aioli de garbanzos, 7

Chile(s): in aji amarillo salsa, 23; ancho, 145; with braised oxtail, 145; catarina, 60; chipotle, 195; in harissa sauce, 24–25; in pimientos de padron, **120,** 121; poblano, 88

Chipotle: chiles, 195; -mustard vinaigrette, 16; espresso-, sauce, 22; grilled lobster with, -mustard vinaigrette, 154; grilled quail with espresso-, sauce, **152,** 153; in posole clam chowder, 48

Chocolate: double, -espresso flourless torte, **170,** 171; steamed, cake, 157

Chorizo: -potato empanadas, **92,** 98–99; cod with clams and, 150

Chowder, posole clam, 48

Chorizo, 195

Cilantro paste, 18

Cinnamon: in pollo harissa, 115; in roasted duck with Moroccan carrot sauce, **146,** 147. *See also* Canela

Citrus: achiote, -steamed chicken in banana leaf, 118; -wine-flavored ice, 167

Clam(s): posole, chowder, 48; steamed in sherry with fennel seed, 111; cod with, and chorizo, 150

Cloves, in pollo harissa, 115

Cocoa toasts, sugared, 168

Coconut rice pudding, sweet, 169

Cod with clams and chorizo, 150

Compote: compota de manzanas y vino, 20

Condiment: compota de manzanas y vino, 20; curry oil, 32; mojo verde, 18; Moroccan olive pesto, 9; paprika oil, 33; pickled red onions, 19

Cookies: icing for, 174; milagro sugar, 173

Corn vinaigrette, sweet, salmon ceviche with, 66

Cosecha, 189

Couscous: Mediterranean salad, 67

Cream: in pernod saffron sauce, 28; in steamed black mussels with carrots and jamon serrano in a Dijon-sherry sauce, **124,** 125

Crianza, 189

Croquetas: salt cod potato cakes, 108; smoked salmon potato cakes, 107

Croutons, 34

Cumin: almond-crusted seared tuna with toasted, tomato sauce, 85; pepita-crusted salmon with toasted, tomato sauce, **138,** 139; in roasted duck with Moroccan carrot sauce, **146,** 147; toasted, tomato sauce, 27

Curry: in chicken salad with celery and grapes, 71; oil, 32

Custard: lavender goat's milk flan, 165; lemon-rosemary flan, 162, **163**


### D

Dates: Mascarpone-stuffed figs and, 158, **159**

Dijon-sherry cream sauce, **124,** 125

Dressing: goat cheese, 61. *See also* Vinaigrettes

Drinks: carajillo, 184; melon mezcalito, 181; nectar of the gods, 177; red sangria, **178,** 179; sangrita oyster shooters, **182,** 183; siesta El Farol, 185; white sangria, 180

Duck, roasted, with Moroccan carrot sauce, **146,** 147

Dulce de Membrillo, 196

## E

Eggplant, Moroccan, 77
Eggs, in tortilla española, **78**, 79–80
Empanadas: Argentine beef, **90**, 91, **92**, 93; baked oyster and pancetta, **92**, 94–95; chorizo-potato, **92**, 98–99; portobello-Cabrales, **92**, 96–97
Espresso: double chocolate-, flourless torte, **170**, 171; -chipotle sauce, 22; grilled quail with, -chipotle sauce, **152**, 153

## F

Fabada, 43
Fennel: clams steamed in sherry with, seed, 111; orange-, olive salad, 76; salsa verde with, seed, 35
Fig(s): aioli de higos, 6; port-, syrup, 26; Cabrales-stuffed, 89; Mascarpone-stuffed, 158, **159**
Fino, 191
Fish: caldo pescado, **44**, 45; stock, 39
Flan: lavender goat's milk, 165; lemon-rosemary, 162, **163**
Fritters, goat cheese and ham, 106

## G

Garbanzos, aioli de, 7
Garlic: in aioli de garbanzos, 7; in basic aioli, 4; in chilled almond, soup, 52; in migas, 34; in patatas bravas, **128**, 129; in romesco sauce, 30, **31**; sautéed, shrimp with lime and Madeira, 84
Garnacha, 189
Gazpacho, **50**, 51

## Ginger

Ginger, in aioli de higos, 6
Goat cheese: dressing, 61; El Farol, tart, 160–61; and ham fritters, 106; preserved lemon, spread, 72
Goat's milk flan, lavender, 165
Granita, 166
Gran Reserva, 189
Grape(s): crispy fried, leaves, 119; curried chicken salad with celery and, 71; salad with fresh mozzarella, **62**, 63
Green onion butter, 8

## H

Ham: Asturian white bean stew with chorizo, blood sausage, and, 43; goat cheese and, fritters, 106. *See also* Jamon
Harissa sauce, 24–25; chicken with, 115; lamb with, 148, **149**
Honey-caper shrimp, grilled, **100**, 101

## I

Ice, citrus-wine-flavored, 167
Icing, 174
Idiazabel, 195

## J

Jamon serrano, 196; watermelon wrapped in, **56**, 57; Cabrales-stuffed fresh figs wrapped in, 89; in queso fresco, 73; steamed black mussels with carrots and, in a Dijon-sherry cream sauce, **124**, 125; trout wrapped in, 140
Jamon stock, 38
Jicama with lime and catarina chile, 60

## L

Lamb, 148, **149;** meatballs with piñon and mint, 103

Lavender goat's milk flan, 165

Lemon(s): -caper aioli, 5; El Farol preserved, 12; preserved, butter sauce, 13; preserved, goat cheese spread, 72; -rosemary flan, 162, **163**

Lime: ceviche, 64; jicama with, and catarina chile, 60; sautéed garlic shrimp with, and Madeira, 84

Lobster, grilled, with chipotle-mustard vinaigrette, 154

## M

Madeira, 84

Manchego, 83, 164, 195; fried pastry filled with quince paste and, 164

Manzanilla, 110, 191

Marcona almonds, 52, 196

Marinades: for lamb, 148; for octopus, 105; for olives, 69; for pork tenderloin, 142; for quail, 153; for roasted duck, 147

Marinated dishes: El Farol preserved lemons, 12; grilled whole pork tenderloin, 102; olives, **68,** 69; Peruvian purple potatoes, 70; red onions, 19; shrimp escabeche with black olives and mint, **74,** 75

Marmitako, 46

Mascarpone-stuffed figs and dates, 158, **159**

Mayonnaise. *See* Aioli

Mediterranean dishes: couscous salad, 67; grilled honey-caper shrimp, **100,** 101; orange-fennel-olive salad, 76; preserved lemon goat cheese spread, 72; sautéed spinach with raisins, 83

Mezcal tequila, 181

Migas, 34

Milagro sugar cookies, 173

Mint: lamb meatballs with piñon and, 103; shrimp escabeche with black olives and, **74,** 75

Morcilla, 195

Moroccan: carrot sauce, 21; eggplant, 77; harissa sauce, 24–25; olive pesto, 9; roasted duck with, carrot sauce, 21, **146,** 147; -spiced swordfish skewers, 110

Mozzarella: grape salad with fresh, **62,** 63; in queso fresco, 73

Mushrooms: portobello-Cabrales empanadas, **92,** 96–97; portobellos en jerez, **86,** 87

Mussels: chilled black, in vinaigrette, 58; steamed black, with carrots and jamon serrano in a Dijon-sherry cream sauce, **124,** 125

Mustard: chipotle-, vinaigrette, 16; grilled lobster with chipotle-, vinaigrette, 154

## O

Octopus, 114; pulpo asado, **104,** 105

Oil: curry, 32; paprika, 33

Olive(s): green, vinaigrette, 14; Moroccan, pesto, 9; marinated, **68,** 69; orange-fennel-, salad, 76; shrimp escabeche with black, and mint, **74,** 75

Oloroso, 191

Omelet: tortilla española, **78,** 79–80

Onion(s): green, butter, 8; pickled red, 19

Orange(s): Mascarpone-stuffed figs and dates with, 158, **159;** -fennel-olive salad, 76; polenta almond cake, 166

Oxtail, 145

Oyster: baked, and pancetta empanadas, **92,** 94–95; -potato soup, 47; sangrita, shooters, **182,** 183

## P

Paella: mixta, 134–35, **136;** pork and spinach, 133; shrimp and blood sausage, 137

Pancetta: baked oyster and, empanadas, **92,** 94–95

Paprika, smoked, 196

Paprika: oil, 33; in cured tuna loin, 59; fresh tuna and potato stew with smoked, 46

Pasta piñon verde, 88

Pastry: El Farol goat cheese tart, 160–61; fried, filled with quince paste, 164

Pecans, in Cabrales-stuffed fresh figs, 89

Pedro Ximenez, 191; caramel sauce, 172

Pepitas, 196

Piquillo peppers, 196

Pepitas, 122; -crusted salmon with toasted cumin tomato sauce, **138,** 139

Pernod saffron cream sauce, 28

Pesto, Moroccan olive, 9

Pimientos de padron, **120,** 121

Pinchos, 36

Pine nuts: in lamb meatballs with piñon and mint, 103; in pasta piñon verde, 88

Pistachios: Mascarpone-stuffed figs and dates with, 158, **159**

Poblano chile, in pasta piñon verde, 88

Polenta almond cake, orange, 166

Pork: grilled marinated whole, tenderloin, 102; and spinach paella, 133; tenderloin with apples and Cabrales cheese, 142, **143**

Port-fig syrup, 26

Portobello: -Cabrales empanadas, **92,** 96–97; en jerez, **86,** 87

Posole clam chowder, 48

Potato: chorizo-, empanadas, **92,** 98–99; fresh tuna and, stew with smoked paprika, 46; oyster-, soup, 47; salt cod, cakes, 108; marinated Peruvian purple, 70; in patatas bravas, **128,** 129; smoked salmon, cakes, 107; in tortilla española, **78,** 79–80

Pudding, sweet coconut rice, 169

## Q

Quail, grilled, with espresso-chipotle sauce, **152,** 153

Quince paste, fried pastry filled with, 164

## R

Raisins, sautéed spinach with, 83

Reserva, 189

Rice, 133; sweet coconut, pudding, 169

Romesco sauce, 30, **31**

Rosemary: lemon-, flan, 162, **163;** -yogurt flatbread, 122; sweet pea, soup, 49

Royal Icing, 174

## S

Saffron, 196; vinaigrette, 15; pernod, cream sauce, 28

Salad(s): curried chicken, with celery and grapes, 71; Mediterranean couscous, 67; grape, with fresh mozzarella, **62,** 63; orange-fennel-olive, 76

Salmon: ceviche with sweet corn vinaigrette, 66; pepita-crusted, with toasted cumin tomato sauce, **138,** 139; smoked, potato cakes, 107

Salsa: aji amarillo, 23; Mediterranean, 29; verde with fennel seed, 35

Sangria, 167; white, 180; sangre del diablo, 33; red, **178**, 179

Sardines, grilled fresh Portuguese, 112, **113**

Sauces: aioli de garbanzos, 7; basic aioli, 4; Cabrales butter, 10; caramel, 172; Dijon-sherry cream sauce, **124**, 125; espresso-chipotle sauce, 22; green onion butter, 8; harissa, 24–25; lemon-caper aioli, 5; Moroccan carrot sauce, 21; pernod saffron cream sauce, 28; port-fig syrup, 26; preserved lemon butter sauce, 13; romesco, 30, **31;** saffron vinaigrette, 15; sofrito, 3; toasted cumin tomato sauce, 27

Sausage: in Asturian white bean stew, 43; shrimp and blood sausage, 137

Scallop ceviche, bay, 65

Seafood: almond-crusted seared tuna with toasted cumin tomato sauce, 85; baked oyster and pancetta empanadas, **92**, 94–95; bay scallop ceviche, 65; ceviche, 64; chilled black mussels in vinaigrette, 58; clams steamed in sherry with fennel seed, 111; cod with clams and chorizo, 150; cured tuna loin, 59; grilled fresh Portuguese sardines, 112, **113;** grilled honey-caper shrimp, **100**, 101; grilled lobster with chipotle-mustard vinaigrette, 154; Moroccan-spiced swordfish skewers, 110; oyster-potato soup, 47; pepita-crusted salmon with toasted cumin tomato sauce, **138**, 139; posole clam chowder, 48; salmon ceviche with sweet corn vinaigrette, 66; salt cod potato cakes, 108; sangrita oyster shooters, **182**, 183; sautéed garlic shrimp with lime and Madeira, 84; shrimp and blood sausage, 137; shrimp escabeche with black olives and mint, **74**, 75; smoked salmon potato cakes, 107; steamed black mussels with carrots and jamon serrano in a Dijon-sherry cream sauce, **124**, 125; stew, 141; trout wrapped in jamon serrano, 140

Sherry, 191; amontillado, in chilled almond garlic soup, 52; clams steamed in, with fennel seed, 111; in Pedro Ximenez caramel sauce, 172; in portobellos en jerez, **86**, 87; steamed black mussels with carrots and jamon serrano in a Dijon-, cream sauce, **124**, 125; in vinagre de jerez, 17

Shrimp: and blood sausage, 137; escabeche with black olives and mint, **74**, 75; grilled honey-caper, **100**, 101; sautéed garlic, with lime and Madeira, 84

Sofrito, 3

Soup: chilled almond garlic, 52; gazpacho, **50**, 51; oyster-potato, 47; sweet pea rosemary, 49; fish, **44**, 45

Spice: El Farol pincho, mix, 36

Spinach: pork and, paella, 133; sautéed, with raisins, 83

Spread: preserved lemon goat cheese, 72. *See also* Sauces

Stew: seafood, 141; Asturian white bean, 43; fresh tuna and potato, with smoked paprika, 46

Stock: jamon, 38; chicken, 37; fish, 39

Sugar: cookies, 173; simple syrup, 179, 180

Sweet pea rosemary soup, 49

Swordfish skewers, Moroccan spiced, 110

Syrup: port-fig, 26; simple, 179, 180


T

Tart, El Farol goat cheese, 160–61

Tempranillo, 189

Tequila, 177; mezcal, 181

Toasts, sugared cocoa, 168

Tomato: almond-crusted seared tuna with toasted cumin,